# EVERYTHING YOU'VE BEEN TOLD ABOUT
# LOVE, SEX
*&*
# MARRIAGE
## IS B.S.

———•————————————•———

*How Couples That Stray Together,
Stay Together*

# Contents

# Living the Fairy-tale

*"To the world you may be one person; but to one
person you may be the world"*
*Dr Suess*

*L*ife is a journey and an adventure with no guarantee that you or I will "live happily ever after". I can promise you though, that if you are not "the world" to the one person you love, and they are not "the world" to you, then the sun will set on your life together long before the sun sets on your own.

Loving someone is loving all of them and that includes their real self and the way they behave naturally in their public, private and sexual lives.

Even if you understand the first two, it is amazing how few people acknowledge or understand that we also have a Sexual Personality and we will either express it or suppress it all throughout our lives. If we supress, hide or display our Sexual Personality in the wrong place then the "Happily Ever After" Fairy Tale may just slip away. Sexual personality's, like regular personality's vary dramatically and your partner maybe be highly sexed or have very little interest in sex. It doesn't matter, as long as you are aware of who they are sexually, and you are cool with that.

I wish all of life was innocent, like we were as children, however when puberty arrives, and the primal instinct of reproduction comes along, our Sexual Personality also arrives. To have a happy, healthy and honest life with our partner we need to understand, acknowledge and manage our Sexual Personality rather than behave like it doesn't exist.

If you think about all the sex scandals, both high profile and in your own world, it's simply a case of someone expressing their Sexual Personality in the wrong place and being caught doing it.

In a few short generations we have come from being happy to have our basic needs met to live in a world that offers us almost unlimited variety in nearly every area of our lives. Yet the rules of marriage haven't changed. Marriage is the one of the few areas of life now where we are asked to go backwards. Traditional marriage means the opportunity of sexual variety is taken away from us for the rest of our lives. In your experience how do things work out when people are given something and then have it taken away? Over half of all marriages end in divorce and around 70 percent of married people have played up on their partner at some stage, so I think it is fair to say this system isn't working that well. I am talking about sexual variety here not love because it has been my experience that you can have one true love for your whole of your life. Lust and sexuality are a different ball game. That's what this book is about. How to manage that desire for sexual variety and excitement in a mature and discrete way so the "happily ever after" dream can be a reality in your life.

# Maybe Together We Can Both Make Our Lives A Little Bit Happier

*I* genuinely hope and believe this book will make you a little bit happier and a little bit more relaxed with life. Every book you read says things like "I'm going to change your life blah blah blah" but I am not going to try to sell you on that promise or anything else really. I will be amazed however if you don't look at life and probably end up doing some things differently after reading this. Even if you don't change a thing you'll know more, and you'll realise you're probably doing OK and will therefore be more relaxed about love, sex and marriage I believe. If you don't break up a happy marriage over sex after you have read this book, then we'll both be very happy. That's what this book is all about – not letting sex interfere with a happy marriage and life. To make that happen you need to lighten up and put sex into perspective. If you do that, I promise your life will change for better, and forever.

## It's all about you (but not in a selfish way)

I have written this book as an anonymous author for two reasons. The first is that it's not about me, it's about you, and I am just the messenger. The second is that I have a beautiful life and a happy family and discretion is the reason for that. If this book became well read and the media found out who I was they would portray my wife and I as weirdos, swingers or whatever it was

3

that got the most public interest. It's nothing personal, the media are just desparate for ratings and ad dollars and they can't afford to worry about who they hurt in the process.

## Resist putting a label on this. Instead just think about what it means to you

I went to an event once and they said we'd play a game where we were not allowed to ask people where they lived, what they did for a job, where their kids went to school or what they did for a hobby. The organiser did this to show us that we automatically start to label and categorise people as soon as we meet them by asking these filtering questions. When you read this, you will be tempted to label us as Swingers (we've never been to a swinger's club) or some sort of weirdos yet, if you met my wife and I, chances are you'd guess she was a kindergarten teacher and me probably a counsellor, I think. We don't take drugs, smoke, break the law or run around the streets naked. We are so normal it would probably freak you out if you met us because the old labelling system just wouldn't work. Our private life, like yours, is private so we can do what we want. We don't hurt others and we are not selfish or hedonistic. Rather we just wanted to try to have a better than 50/50 chance of living happily ever after in a loving marriage and we were prepared to think and act outside the normal way of doing things. What is normal anyway?

## Please excuse my Frankness

I am, by nature, a very polite person however in order to give you my raw view and experience of Love, Sex and Marriage I have written this in a completely unfiltered way. I'm not trying to be rude or crude, just imagine me as that voice in your head when you think things, when you are just about to cum, that would shock people if you said them out loud. So maybe you should

4

read this by yourself. Generally speaking, we know so little about these subjects because nobody talks about them out loud and un-filtered. Quite honestly, I am too embarrassed to as well and the people who know (such as prostitutes) rarely show themselves or share their knowledge. Sex in particular is a secret world in our society because no one ever sees it or talks about it publicly. Remember how shocked you were the first time you found out your parents had to have sex to have a baby? As little kids, most of my friends agreed that our folks must have managed to have kids in another way that didn't require sex in their case. We just could not believe a whole world had been hidden from us and that stays that way into adult hood too which is why it's so hard to measure your own knowledge and ability in this area. Uncertainty creates nervousness and fear so the more knowledge the more relaxed and happier you'll be I would suggest.

## Sexual Awareness and respect

Every time I hear about a woman being attacked by a man, sexually or otherwise, it makes me feel ashamed to be a man. Men are, in a primal sense, predators and these animals who attack and hurt women are really displaying their core animal needs in a brutal way. These men are also at the lowest end of the sexual awareness scale. How could anyone hurt or attack someone if they had any level of awareness about the effect they were having on their victim. This book talks about the primal nature of men and women but that is always based from the view of consenting adults. There is no excuse ever to force someone to do anything they do not want to do. A lot of men are repulsive to women because of their lack of sexual awareness (why would you delib-erately be repulsive to people you were trying to attract?). I hope this book makes them more aware of the behaviour that has been turning off women. A lack of understanding about any subject can cause anger and confusion because you can't work out what you're doing wrong. This book will explain things in an honest manner that no one talks about and I hope that will allow people to have less sexual frustration and hopefully that will make our world a little bit safer

## Is love, family and happy relationships above all to you

In my case, family, friends and love are the greatest and most important joys in life and nothing is more important, and if you feel the same way too then what I am going to say may just improve your life in one or more of these areas. I view Sex as a primal animal act, that should be kept in perspective and I would never allow sex or sexuality to threaten or destroy a loving relationship. In fact, that attitude was to change the entire course of my life many years ago. In the early stages of going out with a beautiful young woman, I went overseas, and she slept with another guy when I was away.

On my return she told me what had happened, and she expected me to break up with her because of it. The thing was she had married, as a virgin, at a very young age and had never been with another man. She was recently divorced and so I understood her sexual curiosity would be high. People have a Sexual Personality and I understood she was highly sexed. Her straying made sense to me and didn't surprise me at all. Women sleep with other men often to see if they are attractive to someone other than their long-term partner and she had only been with one guy in her life.

I wasn't thrilled about her sleeping with the other guy but I wasn't worried about it in the scheme of life and so we moved on. I didn't "guilt trip" or distrust her because that is destructive and, as a result of that decision, we have been happily married for many years. Thank goodness I had the sexual experience that

6

I did have as a youth or I could have ruined a beautiful life for myself over a stray fuck. Like I said, it's just an animal act at the end of the day.

## Living by rules that don't work, made by people you don't know

Have you ever thought about how many rules you live by that don't work and are invented by people you don't know ? Very often people who are adamant and judgmental about those rules are hypocrites themselves and so they can't even live by the rules they preach. Life, love and happiness is too important for any of us to blindly believe a lot of really old ideas that just don't work anymore.

## Questioning the accepted rules by accident

When I was a young guy I was very focused on my sport and so was my buddy. We met a girl we both got on with. We told her neither of us had time for a full-time girlfriend so she was wasting her time. We all kept hanging out together so eventually we told her we had time for half a girlfriend and we'd be happy to share her. She thought about it for a while and then she agreed and we all got on great. Like all woman who have 2 lovers at once, she couldn't keep the smile off her face either. Usually something like that happens in an affair and, when that deception is discovered, it's all drama and misery. That's because our society label someone as bad for having more than one lover, so they hide it and usually hurt a lot of people in the process. If we were taught that people having 2 partners sometimes was normal we would never think a thing about it. We accept that drinking alcohol and becoming mentally incapacitated is normal just because we have been taught that drinking is OK. It's seems it's more about what is socially accepted than anything else in our society.

7

## Doing whatever works for the two of you sexually speaking

My wife and I are honest above all else – which doesn't mean we go crazy or even have an open marriage – which we don't and never will. We just act naturally. In our case, when I met her, my sexual adventures were basically all over but hers were unchartered territory and were confined to one other man in her life. In our case she has had more male partners during our marriage than I have had female partners simply by virtue of her almost nonexistence sexual experience when we got together. If you study history, you will see many famous and successful people have not lived by the norm of a typical married life and I am sure many others who are not famous have too. Like many areas of life, the people at the top create rules for the masses whilst living by an entirely different set of rules for themselves. I am not suggesting you do anything except ask yourself what works for you, regardless of the traditional rules you have been taught about love, sex and marriage.

## Times have changed – have your beliefs?

Beliefs are more important than reality, which is amazing when you think about it, but true. You weren't born with the fear of a blue flashing light, for example, but when you're driving, and you see that light following behind you the stress is real because you have attached a learned meaning to it.

Intelligence doesn't make things any better either, if you have the wrong beliefs, you'll still make the wrong conclusions and, in most cases, the wrong decisions too.

Beliefs and awareness create your destiny and a bit of intelligence doesn't hurt either.

A great deal of our beliefs is developed when we are kids and that is why great achievers often have very powerful role models as children, often their mothers, because we accept most things we are told without judgement as children.

All my life one of my number one desires has been to have a happy healthy family unit and I was prepared to do whatever it took to give myself the best chance of achieving that including questioning the whole premise of marriage and relationships.

My early education in sexuality allowed me to see the reality of sexuality compared to the beliefs we were taught, and I created my own new set of beliefs based on my experiences.

In a world where half of all marriages end in divorce, I was certainly prepared to look at why marriage and partnerships had such a huge failure rate. In other words, I wanted a better than 50/50 chance of making it and I knew those were my chances going down the regular path to an attempt at lifelong bless.

The basis of trust is honesty, so I was determined to create an environment where my partner and I could always be honest. We both felt honesty was more important to us than trying to live by a set of rules that were almost certain to fail, in terms of our sexuality anyway.

## What has "Good" or "Bad" got to do with sexual experience?

We have been brought up from day one to associate sex with many unrelated activities, – it's amazing. I have always been blown away by the fact that someone is described as a, "good girl", if she doesn't sleep with a lot of guys. What has, "good", got to do with your sexual activity? In fact, people have a Sexual Personality, as well as a regular personality, and sometimes that means they are outgoing and adventurous, and sometimes they are quiet and very private. If you are defined as, "good", if you have limited sexual activity does that mean you can, for example, lie, cheat and steal but if you're a virgin you're a good girl? Sex is just a biological need and an animal act. In the cave man days people would have fucked like animals as part of their natural life. They probably would not have eaten with very good table manners either. There is nothing wrong with becoming more sophisticated in our behaviour, however, like most things in life now, it's so complicated and distorted it's frightening. Having more sexual freedom doesn't mean you'll fuck everyone, just like having the freedom to eat anytime you want doesn't mean you will eat until you explode. Our ability to have food whenever we want it just takes away the desperation and focus our ancestors had when they had to go out and hunt for their food. Equally if you know, as an adult, sex is available when you want it then the desperation goes, and sexuality can be brought into perspective as the relatively minor part of our life it should be.

## Living the dream of being together forever

I love hearing about people who were childhood sweethearts and have been together their whole life and with no one else. I didn't have that Sexual Personality as a youngster and had to experiment and there is nothing wrong with either of those sexual personalities. Some people have a high sex drive and some people have a low sex drive. Some people like multiple partners, same sex partners or all sex partners, but what has that got to do with anyone else in their day to day lives unless they are having sex in public, hurting innocent people or imposing their will on others?

But if you impose a huge number of rules and conditions around Sex and Death then you also gain a huge amount of power over people convinced that they may go to Hell if they do the wrong thing. The clever part about these rules is they are largely unrealistic and unable to be abided by so nearly everyone will do something "wrong", feel guilty and therefore be able to be managed and controlled by supposedly doing the, "wrong thing", – think about that. Throughout history, powerful organisations have used guilt and fear to control the masses. Thankfully these days we are free to question everything.

I challenge you to think about whether feeling guilty about sexuality is serving a positive purpose in your life and to ask yourself how much happier you would be if you just looked it as a physical act that only has meaning if you choose to apply meaning to it.

# Sex

## Sex is an urge, but love can last forever

$\mathcal{T}$he truth is that pretty well everything you have been told about love, sex and marriage up to this point in your life has probably been bullshit.

The first biggest load of B.S. is that love and sex are somehow fully connected to each other; not true.

Sex is an urge and the moment it is satisfied you lose interest. Love however is consistent. Would you hug your partner, your child or your dog for a few minutes for example and then feel satisfied and lose interest?

Any man can walk into a room in the dark and within 3 minutes be having sex with a woman he doesn't even know. Can you honestly say that you could fall in love with someone in the dark in 3 minutes without even talking to them? Does the hooker and the client fall in love with each other at every session? I am not knocking having sex with someone you love because it's great. The thing is though, doing almost anything with someone you love is great. Sex and love are totally different emotions and instincts though.

It would be romantic and beautiful if sex wasn't on the agenda in life because it could be just like a romance movie, however in real life, Prince Charming will eventually ask if he can fuck his girl up the bum and cum in her mouth. If you have just shown a shocked look on your face that demonstrates the weirdness in the way we view sex because you've either done both those things, asked to do them, or definitely thought about doing them, so it's weird you should feel shocked at all by that don't you think ?

Not understanding that sex and love are very different is why there are so many broken-hearted women in the world. They confuse sex with love and think it means something to a guy. It can, but it can also mean he has a load of semen he has to get out of his body, and that's an instinctive behaviour ladies, so he is going to release that in one way or another. It's up to the man about the way he manages those needs, but they are all driven by primal urges, if they weren't then the human race would literally cease to exist.

At a primal level, all women have the ability to take on a group of men, simply because the more sperm they get inside them then the more chance they have of getting pregnant. This is primal stuff but true, all ladies reading this please stop reading this now if you have never masturbated to the fantasy of a group of men having their way with you. It's Ok, no one is looking so you can keep reading and your secret is safe with me about the Gang Bang fantasy.

13

## Sex and Innocence

There is a slightly sad and slightly funny joke about the loss of innocence that goes like this.

A teacher walked behind the shed at school to find a 10-year-old boy smoking a cigarette. She warned him that this first cigarette could be the beginning of a life time of bad health. The boy told her that this was far from his first cigarette and that his first smoke was on the night he lost his virginity. The teacher was shocked and asked him at what age he lost his virginity. He told her he was 8 years old. Curiosity overcame shock and she asked "What was it like to lose your virginity at 8 years old?" and he said "To be honest I was too drunk to remember".

I didn't lose my virginity at 8 years old but I had done pretty well everything a boy could do to a girl before I was 15 and it wasn't that big a deal where I was brought up. I won't go into the gory details here but I will talk about my adventures when they are relevant in the story.

In fact I would say my sex life was probably more natural than most people because I learnt about sex without all the rules and prejudices (both reasonable and crazy) that human beings have associated with sex.

When you consider we are the only creatures that do not act naturally about sex perhaps that's why so many people are messed up about it, and, obsessed with it. And boy are people obsessed with it. For example, the combined cost of buying the internet domains names Porno.com, Porn.com and Sex.com was over $30 Million. Yet casino.com on the other hand only sold for $5.5 Million. When you consider sex is not openly marketed or promoted as a product that's pretty impressive. The amazing thing about sex is that our education about it is through pornos, half-truths, hearsay or some dodgy movie at school with all your school mates or worse, your parents, there – kill me now – how embarrassing. Is it any wonder we have a natural interest in that hidden area of life.

It is also not a surprise that most people take sex far too seriously, simply because most of us tend to be over dramatic in areas we lack experience and knowledge in. The thing about sex though is, it's like our other primal urges. Sex is only something people obsess about when they are deprived of it. If we were deprived of food then we would start obsessing about that too, because it's a primal need and part of the survival instinct, as is sex.

## Sexuality is trivial but primal

Is sexuality trivial, well yes and no, it's not trivial if you're starving for something you crave week after week, year after year. Just like food – the hungrier you get the more desperate and focused you get.

My point is that nearly everyone I have ever met, apart from some buddies of mine who shared my childhood, have basically no idea about sexuality and, therefore are usually half starved and semi frustrated in that area, so it takes a more dominant position in their life than it should. If can you get sex, when you want it, or you even know you can if you want it, then sex will no longer be that bigger deal in your life.

Imagine, if for example, you woke up every day with not enough food to eat. How much of your day would you think about food if you hadn't eaten? A lot of the day, right? However, the moment you had something to eat that desire would be gone and you'd then be able to focus on less primal instincts.

The primal instincts come first and one of our core primal instincts is sex. Sex is not an "Optional extra" it's a primal need and the desire is beyond our realm of control. I am not saying you can't control your sex drive just like I am not saying you can't control your behaviour when you are hungry. However, in both cases the longer you go without it the more primal and anti-social you become about getting it.

## Sex - go all the way and come back

Do you remember when you first started learning to drive a car? The concentration required to do everything was incredible and you took it so seriously. A few years later you probably drive along talking on the phone, eating a sandwich and listening to the radio all at the same time. I am not suggesting driving like that, but I am saying that as you become more experienced and more knowledgeable about anything then you know which parts of that activity to take seriously and which parts you can be relaxed about. Even though, for example, you may do all those things in your car you would still stop at all the traffic lights and obey the road rules because that's serious.

Now think about the areas in your life that you take too seriously and then the ones you are confident and cruisy about. I can guarantee that the more knowledge and experience you have on any subject the more confident and capable you are in managing that area of your life. It's the same with sex. If you and your partner have very little experience sexually then you will inevitably take things way too seriously and even break up your relationship over something sexual when you may be perfectly suited in every other way. Sharing fantasies and, where it is private and appropriate, living those fantasies will create more intimacy between you whereas not sharing them or perhaps sharing them with someone else is quite often the beginning of the end and the start of a double life. You will find when you do share your fantasies that sex and sexuality is not the "be all and end all" of life.

My girl and I have no embarrassment about doing anything

together and all that BS about the size of a guy's dick or the staying power of a guy, orgasms or what a woman has to do to please a man becomes basically irrelevant and no big deal because you know it doesn't matter. Sure, you'd love the perfect sexual partner like everyone wants the perfect partner in other ways but "everyone wants a tailored made partner in an off the rack world" and it just doesn't work that way. So, if you base the future of your long-term relationship on the size of a guy's dick or a woman's tits or how long someone can screw for then it's not going to turn out well. Once you become comfortable with sexuality and you have the primal needs under control then the ironic thing is you will go back and focus on relationships and intimacy – bizarre but true.

Having said that, the primal need for sex keeps our species alive so it's a very serious business that must be addressed because no man or woman can ignore it. They may, through discipline and denial, divert it, suppress it, or contain it but it is below regular human thought – it's an instinct not a thought.

## Don't trust lust

A simple way to understand the difference between primal needs and long-term values is that a you will lose interest in a primal need the moment it is satisfied. So what I am saying to you is "don't trust lust". Personally, I don't trust any primal desires; rather I manage them so I can act in a civilized, well, behaved manner. People, (almost always men), who don't satisfy those needs in the right place cause a huge amount of trouble in this world simply because they don't understand the difference between primal and non-primal needs. Love is not something you devote a couple of hours of your time to and then lose interest in. Sex on the other hand, will go from being the number one focus in life to total disinterest within seconds after having an orgasm.

## Prohibition and adultery have a lot in common

Probably one of the dumbest ideas in the history of the free world was prohibiting the sale of alcohol throughout America in what was called the Prohibition era. The marriage system in our modern world today is in many ways suffering the same fate. A group of people in the U.S. decided to ignore the fact that alcohol was (unfortunately) a very strong need for many. When alcohol was made illegal in America all it did was make the average honest person a lawbreaker. The desire for alcohol was stronger than the desire to abide by the new laws introduced at that time. In our society now, we are offered a huge amount of variety in every part of our life. Then the day we are married we are expected to regress back to having no sexual variety for the rest of our life. Just like prohibition, our rules about marriage end up having law abiding citizens breaking the laws of marriage. Honest people deceive their partners simply because the rules about marriage are not in tune with all the variety we can choose in every other part of our life.

## Life, death, sex and confidence

If you have ever spent any time with people who deal with the start of life (sex) or the end of life (death) you may have noticed that they are a lot more fearless and relaxed about things than most people. My experience has shown that if you hang around with Hookers and Ambulance officers there's good chance, you'll have a good time. I am not suggesting that you do anything about confronting death, but I do know if you lose the fear of sex, you'll be far happier and more relaxed. If you haven't had much experience why not go to a professional (male/female prostitute) with your partner and just try anything you like. I am not talking about being kinky, but I am saying if you watch your partner fuck or get fucked and share that experience with them you will actually find it's not that big a deal if there is no love or

18

attachment involved.

It's human nature to be over serious about things we don't understand and are not confident in because we don't have any parameters to judge things by. Think about the first time you tried anything and how nervous and unsure you were. Then think about how you were once you have had a bit of experience. Confident is gained through repetition and experience over time.

It's the same with sex. My girl and I are a super normal fun regular couple yet to outsiders it may seem strange when I ask her if she'd like to go out to the pictures and some dinner next week or if I can arrange her to play around with another guy.

I like watching her play around with other men once in a while and I like her being the centre of attention with one or more men. It's a wild, dirty, fun night and it's also safe and harmless. I adore my girl and she adores me but after 20 years I have no hope of exciting her with my cock as much as the new guy with the new cock does with a new fuck. I don't worry about it either because we don't know these guys, but they all have one thing in common – when they cum they lose interest. Women have a primal enjoyment in being enjoyed sexually and my girl can enjoy that without that terrible feeling a single woman has of being tricked into giving her body away on false pretences. When we go out the only thing, I want that guy to do is fuck my girl and that's why we are there. I don't want him to take her out to dinner or get too friendly I just want him to pound her pussy. The dirty part of life is that when my girl gets fucked by a new guy her pussy is so wet it is impossible for her deny her body doesn't enjoy it and I am glad she does because she's a very happy woman for the next couple of weeks and that's when all our friends ask how she stays looking so young and vibrant. Simple - she is on the stray dick diet and that's a diet that helps her stay fit because the female instinctively cares about looking good for a new partner and will preen and prepare herself far more than she does for me. I don't mind because she looks fantastic and has a charisma about her when she fucks another man that is so powerful it blows my mind.

Of course, I would hate all that if I didn't know the guy would cum and then lose interest. The ultimate fuck for a guy is to fuck, cum and leave with no hassles.

I am not trying to demean the importance of sex, but I am saying that you should try fucking together without any deception with people you don't know and as soon as the fuck is over be able to walk away and never see those people again. If you like them, you might have a return visit but if not, my girl has had a dirty adventure and I know I'll get great sex for the next couple of weeks. Additionally, the guys are happy because they have had a no strings attached fuck with a hot new woman – it's all good

Just like any other area of a happy marriage, you should be attentive to your partner and the situation, as we both are with each other. I rarely sleep with other women because I had done pretty well everything before I met my partner (yes, I am older) whereas she had done pretty well nothing. If the tables were turned, I would have had a lot more sex because I would have been the one who was curious and inexperienced.

## Being sexually bored and the "Coolidge Effect"

In 1958 behavioural endocrinologist Frank A. Beach did tests on rats about sexual variety and coined the phrase "the Coolidge Effect" named after EX US President Coolidge and a joke about sexual disinterest.

The presidential couple go to a chicken farm and Mrs Coolidge notices that a Rooster is mating with the chickens continuously.

She asks the assistant if the rooster is always that active. The assistant tells her the rooster is. President Coolidge then asks, "is it always with the same chicken?" to which the assistant replies "Oh no sir that lucky rooster gets almost unlimited variety" President Coolidge looked at his wife and said "I rest my case"

You can read all about the experiments of Doctor Beach or I can summarise by saying that a rat had sex with all the rats in his cage then lost interest. Every time they introduced a new rat his interest returned, and he regained his energy and interest and had sex with the new rat. The doctor proved it is a physiological condition – we are naturally designed to spread our seed around. The great news is that apparently this is not the case with Crickets or Penguins so ladies, if you are open minded, I could set you up with a faithful partner for life if you like. Incidentally they do say the difference between a rat and a man is that when you give six drinks to a rat it doesn't turn into a man!

## Being labelled a cheater is the start of the end of a marriage

The term "cheating" is so denigrating and shameful. When you consider over 70% of men have slept with a prostitute and Ashley Madison (the dating site for people who want to play up on their married partner) has over fifty-one million subscribers worldwide I think maybe we need to update our thinking about marriage and sex– wouldn't you agree?

I am an absolute supporter of marriage and the family unit, but today's marriage is in the same structure as it was hundreds of years ago when people lived to their mid-30's and only travelled a few miles away from home. The world has changed but the expectations of married couples hasn't and around half of all marriages don't work because of the same unrealistic expectations as Prohibition I would suggest.

The modern marriage takes two perfectly honest, good people and then, if either play up, it makes them into liars and cheats even though that's often not their nature. Just like Prohibition, their primal need for sexual variety has made nice honest people compromise themselves and that's what a great number of married people go through, it's crazy.

Sex, Trust and Respect are very different things but, with our current old-fashioned expectations on marriage, perfectly good people inadvertently humiliate each other and lose faith in each other often ending in another broken couple and broken family unit. So many lives are ruined because of an inability in married couples to discretely manage the primal desire in men and women for sexual variety. It's insane, sad and completely unnecessary

Even if couples don't break up over an affair the level of trust is less, and the happiness and comfort has been lowered too in the relationship.

## It's not the sex it's the intimacy that dooms marriages

The other problem with people having to secretly have other sexual partners is it can create intimacy which can also lead to a break-up of the original marriage because the new person has new stories and is interesting just by the fact that they are new. In the long term though they won't be new anymore and may not be suited anyway. It's easy to confuse new with love. So, the first thing that needs to be done is to separate honesty and trust from a sexual animal act. Trust takes years to build but two people can fuck in a minute without even knowing each other's name. That's why sex and love shouldn't be viewed in the same way and probably why the Hollywood marriages are so often short lived there.

# Sexual Personalities – the hidden side of us all

If you don't understand and acknowledge your partners Sexual Personality, then you don't really know them. That's why one day someone is shocked to find a whole other side to their partner when that person has been having an affair, seeing prostitutes are bisexual or whatever.

Guys, if you have seen some sweet little woman with a knuckle dragging ape of a man, or ladies, if you have seen an intelligent, nice guy with an airheaded bimbo, then the chances are they are together because they suit each other's Sexual Personality. If you don't understand the Sexual Personality of your partner, then you only know a part of that person and, as love should be unconditional, it's important to know all of them. If you don't understand that separate Sexual Personality, then that could be where you have been missing out with partners you want and like because they will never tell you or talk about it. In many cases someone's Sexual Personality can be the opposite of their outward personality. I won't mention the name of the actress, but one popular American actress who played a lot of sweet romantic roles was hooked up with a bikie type, that was knocking off porn stars and hookers while he was with her. She obviously didn't understand that her Sexual Personality was attracted to an animal, so she chose a guy with the outward personality of an animal too which can be a life ruining decision. What she needed was an "adaptive" guy. A man who could be a good honourable person in public and an animal in the bedroom. She would have satisfied both her public and sexual personalities without all the misery. Equally if he was a guy who liked screwing hookers and porn stars, she should have been aware of his Sexual Personality and accepted that or not. If she had accepted that, or otherwise, we would never have known about his behaviour. I would have known immediately that, because people treat this woman like she is the Virgin Mary and butter wouldn't melt in her mouth, she would probably be attracted to someone with raw sexuality. It's the Yin and Yan of life. A lot of people don't understand their Sexual Personality, so they end up with a life of misery because they satisfy that need in an inappropriate way with a person who is unsuited to them in many other ways. The trick is to find someone with your values and beliefs and then cater to each other's Sexual Personality in private and without judgement. The quickest way to know what sort of Sexual Personality someone has is to describe scenarios when you're having sex and whatever makes the other person very hard or very wet – bingo you've hit the jackpot. If what they like is way out of your comfort zone, then you need to try to find a way to compromise. If it's legal and doesn't hurt anyone then maybe you should consider it. You have to be natural and happy though and if you just can't go there it's better to know sooner than later.

## Sexual Personalities are kinky by their very nature

Why do some people like dressing up in S & M gear whilst others like dirty talk, women, men, women and men together and even groups? Some like being humiliated and some like doing the humiliation, some like role playing, fucking in Furby suits or even fighting turns them on. The answer is, "I have no idea". If you love your partner, it doesn't totally freak you out and it's harmless then you should try to accept and understand this side of their life. I will guarantee that if you let them express this private sexual personality with you, it will bond you together in an amazing way. The opposite is true too if you judge them and make them feel bad about themselves. Being judgemental will alienate your partner and they will do what they desire with someone else and that will start separating the intimacy between you and your partner.

## How to keep a partner sexually interested forever

If you are one dimensional and haven't explored or are not aware of your sexual personality, then unfortunately your partner is going to get bored in the bedroom pretty quickly if they are highly sexed. If you're judgemental or critical of your partner, then you'll make them unhappy. If you can't really accept the animalistic and primal side of men or the lustful and erotic side of women, then you just need to find another person with low sex drive and partner up with them. There is absolutely nothing wrong with that. Just be yourself and be natural.

Ladies, men need to fuck, and they can be disgusting but if the sexual side of men turns you off then make no mistake, if you do not satisfy their carnal desires, they will end up fucking other women or they will be angry and resentful. Men are visual, crude and primal too and they want to look at you as a sexual object in the bedroom and use you that way. It may seem childish and crude, but men are programmed in their DNA to find and have sex with women to keep the race going.

The difference between men and women is that women can be very conservative until they're horny, once they are horny though they will do anything. I have got women to do absolutely everything I could possibly imagine when they were horny …provided they have had a recent bikini wax and were wearing nice underwear. It's amazing you can have a woman getting double penetrated whilst a group of guys watch and she's licking a woman's pussy – no problems but you try to get her gear off if she hasn't had a bikini wax – forget it!

So as a woman you need to be, in the right circumstances, a non-judgemental whore for your husband. As a man you need to use your imagination and encourage your women to express herself to you and bring out her inner most fantasy's without judgement on your behalf.

## Don't mention the War (I mean the Whore)

There is a classic Fawlty Towers episode where John Cleese keeps talking about the war to a German couple and he says "Don't mention the war, I mentioned it once, but I think I got away with it"

I discovered long ago that the female race really doesn't understand their own sexuality, and if they do recognise parts of it, they try to ignore it, or they are embarrassed and even angry at what turns them on too. So, guys, never mention the Whore, (that's inside every woman) because she simply cannot handle it and the things she thinks about just before she is going to cum scares and often embarrasses her. She can't even talk about it to herself and almost always, regardless of what she does, she doesn't want to admit it even to herself little own anyone else. It's almost laughable because you basically have to pretend that you don't know what is going to happen when you absolutely do know what's going to happen.

When a guy asks a girl up to his place late at night when they are both boozy and asks "would you like to come up for another drink" he really means "would you like to come up and, if I do everything right and you like me, fuck me tonight". Woman though, don't like to admit they are potentially going up there with that in mind, even though they do have that in mind. If the guys do everything right and they do sleep together then the next day the woman will tell her friends "he invited me up for a drink and one thing led to another". No, what actually happened is that women rule the world, as they should in that way. If she wanted sex, she just had to let the guy know it was OK and she just had to go upstairs for the deed to be done.

So, guys I suggest treating your girl like a whore (in a role-playing sense, respectfully and with her consent of course) in private if she likes it, and I have never met a woman who doesn't. The funny thing is, the more you treat a woman like a whore in private, the more polite and well-mannered you both seem to enjoy being in public, I have found. In fact, this is not a new concept, famous American playwright Wilson Mizner said around 1910, *"Treat a whore like a lady and a lady like a whore"*. She may like a stranger or two to play with her once in a while and, when the time is right, you may even get a bit of girl on girl action because I have never met a girl who won't play with another girl when the time is right, but you can't talk about it because the lady folk are doers not talkers.

## High achievers and sexual personalities

During the Depression in America Napoleon Hill worked for President Roosevelt in the Whitehouse in an attempt to get the economy going again. He asked to be paid $1 a year and wrote a book about creating wealth and anything you want to in life. The book has now sold over 100 million copies.

Chapter 11 in the book is titled "The Mystery of Sexual Transmutation". Transmutation simply means directing drive and energy from one area to another. If you have ever wondered why many high achievers are often exposed having multiple affairs and partners, it is simply because the very nature of achievement comes from sexual drive. These people are less inhibited about sexuality than average society and that is part of why they are not average. They let their sexual energy go, focus a lot of it on achievement and then some on sexuality itself.

## Tune into your primal sexual awareness

It's actually amazing how many people do have sexual awareness, but most don't understand it. There is a hidden world of sexuality out there and you instinctively have that knowledge within you. The more you acknowledge and learn about sexuality in the human animal the more you will be able to take care of your partner's needs and relate to the partner you would like to be with. We have been brainwashed to judge partners on whether we have common interests. When it comes to sexuality though, you need to go back to cave man days and strip that person naked (metaphorically). Pay attention to the primal instincts and the animal without any possessions or status attached. Ladies, if you met a guy at a party and instead of asking "where do you work" you asked "do you think this dress suits me"  and innocently turned around and let him look at your butt (which is called presenting in the animal kingdom) I promise you will get his attention and you will get him thinking in a primal way. If you lower your eyes when you talk to him that is an animal instinct for a hunter (the male) and he will get turned on by his "dominant" position over you). Don't worry, if you do end of together, you'll rule the roost – it's just a short-term thing ladies. It starts though with primal attraction so if you want a primal relationship, then focus on the primal world.

## Ladies - share your pussy but not your heart

In a purely practical sense, women are like Queens Bees and can easily handle 5 or 6 men at a time (and I am not talking maybe there), however conversely, women are simply not suited to sharing their heart around. In fact, I think the number of sexual partners a woman has should just be decided by her and her partner in the privacy of their own little world. I do know, however, the magic number of people a really happy woman will love in her life and that is (drumroll please) - one.

28

Women are romantic, loving and nurturing and they are not suited to sharing their heart around at all, their pussy on the other hand likes variety, lust and the feeling of a new man inside them.

A guy is different because he could just fuck anything that moves and move on if there are no consequences and he is given the freedom to do that. Spoiler alert – Ladies at this point if you said or thought "my guy is not like that" you have a very low level of sexual intelligence. Those primal instincts come in at the ground level of the brain functions along with breathing and eating and if you believe otherwise, you're just kidding yourself.

I am not advocating an open marriage or society however I am suggesting that if you and your partner can be open about your sexuality and you can both handle it then you'll never have to lie and you won't be bored or frustrated, as many long term partners are.

Being bored with having sex with the same person for 20 years doesn't mean you don't love and adore that person, it's just that anything you do the same for many years can be become boring and you shouldn't worry about that. Think about the last time you flicked through the TV remote and looked at multiple programs yet stilled wanted more variety – we humans love variety. Right now, your regular sex life is private and if you keep it that way then you can try new things and never have to wear the consequences if they don't work out.

## Nice guys are animals too

If you're a woman reading this then I am sure, at some stage in your life, you have found it hard to understand how a seemingly nice man can become so crude and animalistic about women and sex. The key word there is animalistic because, for all their refinement in the modern world, men are still animals by nature. Part of the role of the male animal is to procreate and that is not an activity, it's an instinct, and there's a big difference between the two.

I mentioned we are the only animal that does not act naturally, in a sexual sense, but how many times have you really thought about that? The rules we live by now were man made, centuries ago, and a long time before mass travel, mass communication, and the era of almost unlimited choice in everything. People and society have changed beyond recognition since those days, and so have a lot of traditions in society, except our views on Love, Sex, and Marriage. Is it any wonder so many marriages fail?

Marriage is a man-made invention, sleeping with only one partner after you marry is a man-made concept and if people were taught a different set of values, they wouldn't think twice about it.

I mention this because one of the biggest problems we have in our world is broken families and unhappily married people and often unhappy kids too.

To me, happy family units and happy, honest people create the best world we can possibly live in, and yet, because our sexual and marriage rules are so out of touch with the world, we see marriages screw up all the time because of sex and infidelity in a certain amount of those cases.

If you never learn to understand and guide the animalistic side of us ex cave creatures, then you'll never really understand men or women, and you will probably have difficulty keeping a partner in life.

That's what this book is about. Absolutely no BS just an unfiltered look at the male and female sexual animal. You can choose to accept or reject what I have written but either way I guarantee your ability to understand the sexual nature of people will be so much better than it was before because it just never seems to be talked about openly and honestly.

The true sexual nature of men is up there with the Easter Bunny and Santa Claus in terms of something that is a secret kept collectively by the male race for fear of retribution by the women of the world.

You know those guys you meet who are considerate and well-mannered and genuinely care about you and what you have to say in your life. They are the ones who say please and thank you every time when you are working in the service industry and they always treat you with respect even when they are a position of power and don't have to. I am one of those guys. I believe in life that everyone should be respected and treated with decency and that they have an interesting story to tell, and I happen to be one of those people who really wants to hear it. The challenge is that when you read what I have to say here you may be shocked at how direct I am. I mention this because I have to assure you that I am not deliberately trying to upset you with the way I have written it. I just want to give you the absolute unfiltered truth and I think that is more important to be honest and straightforward than it is to be subtle. Honesty will give you the greatest power possible to enable you to judge and test what I say for yourself.

For ladies and men, I really believe that if my experiences can help you become a little more relaxed, happy and confident about handling the opposite sex and their sexuality, then you will be a lot more confident and happier in your life. Remember too that men, as animals, can sniff a lack of confidence a mile off, just like women can with men, and that will make a difference in getting and keeping the partner you want too.   What I do want to do for you is to empower you with a far greater understanding of people and their sexuality than you have right now – because my experience has shown me that most people have no idea about the primal side of men and women and statistically that would suggest that you are probably one of those people.

For ladies for example, it's hard to comprehend that a nice guy can turn into an animal. How can you reconcile charming Hugh Grant as Mr Darcy and then compare that with him being caught in L.A. in his car getting a blow job from a street hooker? So, I can understand why most women (hookers excluded) live in denial about that side of men and the crude animalistic piggish side of our nature. It's just too much to comprehend, and as is typical when a situation is too traumatic to take in, humans simply deny it exists as a defence mechanism. So, women typically manage that horrible concept with the universal line "yes but my guy's not like that". He is though, because If all his male parts work properly then he is genetically designed to reproduce by almost any method possible.

Even though your man is an animal in clothing whose strongest instinctive behaviour is self-preservation and reproduction, do you really believe that he can, by an act of will, rise above his primal instincts. No longer will he feel hunger, he will be above that, no longer will he feel sexual desire, he will be above that too. Ask yourself if that can really be true?

I think you know it isn't true, and that's why 70% of married men have had sex with other women and why brothels and strip clubs have existed since the beginning of time, men have to fuck. You either manage it and keep your guy hanging around forever or you ignore it and let him drift away, be angry or he will get the good stuff somewhere else and live a double life.

Ladies, if you have ever wondered why guys sometimes pick women who don't seem to be that smart or aware or even inter-

32

esting compared to you, then here's why. You look at this guy and see that you have similar views and interests, you like the same movies, books and music, you can really talk to each other so why not you ...right?

The answer is that you are focusing on all the "extras" rather than the primary needs of the man and woman being together.

## Get the primal side right first

Imagine for example going to a restaurant that has a beautiful string quartet playing discretely in the corner, incredible décor, friendly happy staff, the open fire crackling away and then the Maître D comes over and explains they have run out of food.

The restaurant has focused on everything except the primal reason everyone is there, food.

The problem is that you are hungry, and hunger is not an optional extra, it's not something you have to learn, it's something you are programmed with at a level underneath logic or reasoning, you have to eat.

You make a quick exit and head for the Chinese place down the road that has the lingering aroma of beautiful food wafting out of the kitchen. You don't care about the plastic tablecloths, a dodgy interior or even the mildly unpleasant waiters, you just have to have food.

Now replace food for another one of our basic primal needs, sex and sexuality, (not just the act of sex because that's a small part of the whole deal)

If you can't get or keep a partner, it may be because you've been focusing on the wrong things and everything you have been told otherwise is Bullshit. Men want to have sex and be sexual with women first, last and in the middle. Women to a lesser extent because men have to be ready to provide sperm at all times whereas women have to actually create a child when the time is right (in a primal sense that is). Men really are focused primarily on sex at first. Yes, they will get to know you and hear about your family and your life, but above all, their primal instinct and desire is to get you naked and fill you with seed. It's the reproductive instinct, they don't have a choice about desire, it's just there all the time.

Ladies, I am not encouraging you to have sex with every guy on a first date, but I am saying you need to communicate with men, and their sexual nature, if you want to interest and hold a partner. It's sexuality first, the unspoken primal language between man and woman, then everything else later.

Conversely, men need to have the same understanding of female sexuality. I have heard so many guys ask how some big ape can go out with such a sweet girl and the answer is he is consciously or unconsciously appealing to her primal sexual nature and personality. Whenever I meet a sweet innocent looking woman, I know that the sweeter she looks, the wilder her sexual personality is. Sweet women get frustrated by everyone treating them like a they are an angel, and as happens often in life, they often overreact and then go the bad boy root.

As I mentioned before, just like a regular personality, people have sexual personalities too, and you need to accept both personalities if you want a chance of a happy life together. Most sweet women get really frustrated because men want to treat them like angels and ignore their sexual personality. These women may meet a big gorilla who is naturally an animal and they get attracted to that man regardless of the other unsuited sides to his personality which often doesn't work out well.

Most of those magazine articles about men women and sexuality, all those quiz's, so much of that information is written by people who either have no idea what they are talking about or are simply filling the magazine with articles that are acceptable to print. It doesn't matter how smart you are because if you are not being told the right information to base your decisions on you will mess things up. So, if you have ever had someone leave you for someone who couldn't hold a candle to you then that's probably why.

You need to have common values of course however having general interest things in common is a bonus in relationships but not the primary need. I have a lot of things in common with my grandmother but that doesn't mean I want to fuck her. All that matters at the beginning is whether the man or woman relates to you in a sexual way because you are both primal sexual animals and that primal behaviour comes before logic and check lists provided by people desperate to sell magazines. Roger Moore (the famous actor who played James Bond years ago) understood that, when he married an Italian woman before either could speak each other's language. In fact, it was his longest of 4 marriages and lasted over 30 years.

Being sexually attracted to someone doesn't mean that's the right life partner for you but lacking that attraction means it's going to be a struggle right from the "get go" so why bother?

## Fake News

The double standards in the media are breathtaking and insulting too because you are lied to every day. Actions speak louder than words though, and the bullshit stops when the dollars come into play. The networks understand primal needs and cannot afford to ignore them, or they'd go broke.

All the bullshit goes out the door when ratings and dollars

come into the picture, that's why female newsreaders are usually 30-year-old blondes who are "fuckable". An expression I honestly find crude, however that it is the accepted industry term used by executives looking at hiring female on air staff. The cold hard fact is that if you want to be a female newsreader you must be "fuckable". It is the absolute number one criteria in the commercial world of TV. It's understood and vocalised by all the decision makers because the ratings are what they are after above all else.

I have no problem with the hot newsreader (Hey I'd like to fuck her too) but I do have a problem with women being sent out into the world loaded with bullshit and then wondering what's going wrong.

The bullshit never stops either, for example have you ever noticed in the media how people break up because they "don't communicate" or just "grew apart" but they never break up "because they met someone new and exciting after 20 years with the same person". It breaks my heart when people split up with a long-term partner because they don't understand the difference between "lust and newness" which are both unreliable and temporary states, compared to true love and lifelong happiness.

## No sexual boredom or distrust at our house

Everyone does get bored sexually with the same partner, it's a primal instinct to want a new sexual mate (that's why a human's sex drive halves after being with the same person for a year or two), but that doesn't mean you don't love your partner. It's natural to be excited by newness and variety but it should be kept in perspective. I'll talk more on this later, but my wife has one-night stands with other men once in a blue moon just to create a bit of excitement in our lives and we view those nights out like any other adventure we do. Sometimes I sleep with an ex who is single or a married woman with the consent of her husband too. Other times though our big night out is going to the theatre or dinner with friends. It may seem bizarre that we also view a night out for a sexual adventure pretty well the same. Sometimes I arrange for a dinner with a businessman from interstate and after dinner that guy seduces my wife and has sex with her. He goes back to his interstate home; we go home and it's back to normal life the next day. We get our variety out in a controlled way and the chances of us breaking up through boredom or infidelity are absolutely zero. That may sound strange to you, but you have to ask why it is strange to you and the answer is the rules we have been told to abide by. Be honest have you ever really questioned those rules?

With over half of all marriages failing and so much infidelity don't you think they may be worth questioning?

It's interesting that there are so many controlling rules around the greatest primal desire people have (sex) and the greatest primal fear they have (death). What power would these institutions have if you made decisions about who you had sex with based on your own common sense and you just assumed that death was simply a natural end to life with no more to it than that. Imagine a life with no guilt or fear related to sex and death.

In fact, a great number of beliefs that are held in our society about love, sex and marriage simply don't work which results in many innocent people suffering, particularly children when marriages break down.

## Fake News and feeling bad about ourselves

I love the world and I am not cynical by nature so I am not saying the world is bad, I just want to share with you the difference I have experienced between reality, good marketing and organisations using fear and judgement to gain power over you and your life.

Every day we are bombarded in the media with images of perfect families and perfect people when companies are trying to sell us something, make money out of us or control us in some way. Those images and scenarios though are usually Bullshit and they can affect the way we feel about ourselves and how we look at our life.

I live in a world where I have been around the people in media portraying the perfect family stuff and if ever there was a more fucked up bunch of people than most actors and media personality's I haven't met them yet. I know for a fact they make money out of giving the delusion of looking perfect and therefore being better than the average person. If they didn't seem better than you then they wouldn't be paid all that money. I not saying there is any evil intent there that's just the way it is.

Big business and media personalities aren't pulling the wool over your eyes to be wicked or mean they just do whatever has to be done to make money and will tell you any BS they can to get away with it whenever it suits their needs. To me that shows a total lack respect. I can't stand lying and I can't stand pathetic people who lie for their own self-interest. It's childlike and creates sadness and mistrust in our world and I hate that. My aim is not to pick on big business, or anyone else for that matter, but I do need to expose the Bullshit they peddle to you every day so you can rise above that and make decisions based on truth not bullshit.

So, my challenge to you is look at the actions and character of people rather than words and images.

As someone wise once said "your actions are so loud I can't hear the words you're speaking".

Total hypocrisy and bullshit in the media and big business is there because they are not there in business to hold the moral high ground or try to change the core primal instincts of humans, they are there to make money and get ratings. If you want to know the truth about any area just follow the money and the BS stops there. The TV stations need ratings and advertisers. Pussy sells and it makes the money. As Comedian Sir Les Patterson says, "Sweetheart you're sitting on a fortune".  The media need ratings and advertisers to survive so you can watch the fuckable newsreader and then in the ad breaks you can watch the fuckable people in the ads. Sex and sexuality make the world go around and the TV channels don't have the luxury of ignoring that. Like I said I'm not against the TV guys as long as you are aware it's bullshit and don't take it as being real.

## The value of honesty

The commercial world aside, the personal side of dishonesty is soul destroying and confidence sapping and conversely honesty is an absolute turn on and is one of the ultimate forms of showing respect.

Honesty gives the person you are dealing with the ability to make a judgement for themselves with all the facts at hand. I am not talking about a lack of diplomacy or hurtful comments clothed in the excuse of honesty - I mean true honesty. Letting someone know where they stand and doing that with dignity and respect. That's why I don't and won't lie to anybody.

It's both sad and amazing how much misinformation and misguided BS is written about love, sex and marriage and the end result is a huge number of broken homes and marriages, partners playing up, guys fucking hookers on the side, honest people being deceptive and often living double lives to satisfy the sexual side of their being.  If you remove dishonesty about sexual behaviour, I wonder how many good marriages and relationships would have been saved.

## Everybody is a sexual creature so nice girls suck dick (and take it up the bum) too

If ever there was something that showed the curious sexual nature of women, it is anal sex.

I have never ceased to be amazed by meeting the sweetest most innocent looking girl in the world and then if I was lucky enough to become her lover, told her I wanted to fuck her up the bum. She would show a shocked look and then say something like "that's a bit naughty I couldn't do that ... besides, (pause – there's always a pause), last time it hurt".

The point is that we are all sexual and curious so if you go out with a woman and just mount her a couple of times a week and pump away guys then there is a good chance, she is going to be pretty frustrated and bored. I am not talking about being frustrated, in terms of having an orgasm or not, I am talking about frustration because you have a Ferrari at your disposal and you're treating her like a shopping cart.

## Women rarely ever admit they need sex

Maybe it's magic or maybe it's just a coincidence but I have never, ever, ever known a woman admit that she fucked a guy just because she was horny, they are incapable of saying that. Women are genetically designed to BS about fucking, perhaps it's a defence mechanism, but it seems to be part of their DNA. A woman will go out on a girls night, drink straight vodka out of the strippers boot, let him fondle her and then (surprise, surprise) go home with him and get the living daylights fucked out of her with some of that dirty horny fucking that is only that exciting when it's a new stranger, a new scent and a new man inside her. Fast forward to the next morning and now we have one very regretful, shamefaced girl who, now that it's daytime and sober explains why she got boned the night before.

Even when she's single it's because "she was upset about work or felt sorry for the guy or needed a confidence boost blah, blah ,blah" but there is one thing I have never heard come out of a woman's mouth and that is "I was just horny and my pussy ached for cock so I just needed a fuck'. I know women judge each other, but it seems more than that. I think they are genetically geared to lie to others and themselves, and they do it all the time about their sexuality.

It's that timing issue again. Talk dirty to the right girl at the right time and in the right place and you may get lucky. Try it in the cold hard light of day when she is sober, unemotional and focused on the many other parts of her busy life and you'll be branded a pig. If you do act like that inappropriately then the ladies are right. You are a pig, because you have displayed a complete lack of sexual awareness which is one of the greatest faults with men generally speaking. I know I have twisted this quote before but, "sex is all of a man's life but only part of a woman's life" and guys if you get your timing wrong continually then you are a fool.

## Men (boys) with double standards lose big time

What turns people on and why are people so different? Who knows, and why does it matter anyway? Most men will let a woman know what turns them on and sooner or later ask their girl to do it. In fact, it's accepted that men are dirty bastards who are nearly always thinking about sex. Yes, men are animals, I think we've established that.

But what about women? It's been my experience that a lot of men are really messed up, and quite childish, about their view of women. They want to have dirty sex and they want to use a woman like a whore, but they want a vestal virgin as a partner. They can't seem to understand that their woman can be both things at once, depending on the timing and environment. The fantastic thing about that is, that instead of having a double life where they have sex with the occasional Hooker and then have vanilla flavoured sex at home, they can actually enjoy both sides of themselves and their partner If they are honest open and trusting.

The double standard displayed by a great deal of men, understandably, makes women scared of really expressing their deeper most erotic fantasies and dreams because they may be judged and humiliated for them.

A woman will never ever tell a guy this but men with the vestal virgin attitude are, in a certain way, always viewed by women as being boys, because they have never grown up and learnt to enjoy all the incredible parts of women emotionally, romantically and sexually.

The result is that, guys like me, have so many women they can do anything with, whilst these judgemental guys whinge about how hard it is to get women. It amazes me that some men (boys) do something dirty to a woman and then tell all their mates and label her as a slut or dirty bitch. How bizarre and childlike. These "man child's" don't understand that a woman's privacy and reputation is everything and, more than that, how could you do something mean or talk about someone in a mean way when they have been kind, generous and they have trusted you. If a woman has let you have sex with her, it is a privilege that should be respected and appreciated.

It's no wonder women get cynical about men when some men are so fucked up

So, you see while it's acceptable for men to ask for anything, it's a dangerous thing for a woman to do and so she simply won't do it and either wait for some guy to try or remain frustrated in that area.

This comes back to understanding sexual personalities and why sweet girls go out with big gorillas.

Freedom comes through expressing ourselves without judgement. If you have a partner, you can trust and express yourself with sexually then you will both be free in that sense.

## Pussy rules the world so use it for good not evil

Women often act naive and shocked when men talk or suggest sex to them and yet they all fuck and inherently understand that the golden rule is *she who has the pussy (eventually) makes the rules*

In fact, the two distinctive classes of men in the world are those that won't get their balls broken for sex and those who think they have to grovel, beg, buy and lie for it.

Weak, pathetic men are a turn off for women because having a lack of sexual awareness is why those men believe they have to beg and grovel and so they turn women off anyway. Women may accept men like that as a trade-off for a better lifestyle, but men like that frustrate and annoy women, and it's a shame because they may be great guys who just need to become more self-aware.

The key is to act naturally and find a partner who suits you. There are plenty of gentle women, for example, who don't abuse the weak men, it's just when a hard woman is with a soft man it ends in tears and that's the same with a hard man being with a soft woman too. Unfortunately, women particularly, who are attracted to the hard side of men in an animalistic way, often don't understand that the other parts of a hard man are unsuitable for their nature. Men who understand adaptive behaviour, meaning they can be both hard and soft, are the ones who are good for gentle women.

## Sex is ugly and men are pigs

Let's face it, sex can be ugly, and men can be crude pigs when it comes to sexuality because their animal instinct is to have sex with as many women as they can, and they can be disgusting in the way they go about it. I get that, but it's primal so it's not like they have a choice in that desire and it's crazy to think otherwise. They do, however, have the power to control the timing of their behaviour and the person they behave in that way with. Bad timing and a lack of awareness about the receptiveness of the woman are probably the two biggest turns offs for women all over the world.

Luckily, if men choose to be responsible thinking adults, they can learn to behave in a civilised manner. That primal instinct is still there though and is just lurking under the surface waiting to come out if isn't controlled. Remember we humans may have fancied ourselves up a bit but we are still primal animals with the same primal instincts and those instincts are stronger than anything else in our core being.

When I read articles about "changing the nature of males" I can't believe anyone can be that naïve. Ladies if you embrace and believe the "My guy isn't like that" line of thinking then you are creating a barrier between you and your man and he will create a duel personality. I can't tell you how many times I have seen a man have a complete personality change when he is let loose near women and he is away from his partner simply because he can't be honest about sex at home. That's sad because there's a part of him that you'll never know and if you judge him or punish him for being a primal animal, he'll learn to hide that side from you forever. A dog doesn't come when you call him if you beat him every time when he comes back.

If you are judgemental then your partner will start separating parts of their personality from you and that's how distancing starts. Hookers often say that after guys get their rocks off, they talk and talk and talk and I suspect that's because they are dealing with a non-judgemental person and they can be natural and not scared of being punished if they say the "wrong" thing.

Also, once a man has satisfied the primal instinct of sex then you will get a decent conversation out of the guy because he will be able to think properly. Even men get annoyed at how sex dominates their thinking when they have a "full load". It can be frustrating both physically and mentally when you want to focus on other things but find it hard (no pun intended)

If you wanted a great dinner conversation with a guy and said to him "We haven't been together before and I don't want you to think about sex all through dinner so how about I give you a blowjob before we go out so then at least I will get a couple of hours of conversation out of you without sex getting in the way". I am not really saying you should do that but if you did you would be amazed at how relaxed and interesting that guy would be. On the other hand, if he ran away straight after he came then you'd know he was a waste of time anyway.

If the sex part is dealt with in isolation rather than having it combined with secrecy and deception and inevitably intimacy you will be amazed how that will change your life.

## Sex is all about timing, as you know ladies, most men don't get that

One of the greatest conflicts between men and women is

man's obsession with getting sex. The reason men are like that is because, in a primal reproductive sense, all men need to do is provide their seed and they must be ready to do that at all times. Woman on the other hand are not interested in sex a lot of the time and this is where the conflict arises. A man with a heightened sexual awareness understands that being sexual when a woman is not in the mood is a real turn off.

When you hear stories about men exposing themselves, masturbating in front of women and talking suggestively in the wrong context then that just demonstrates that man's total lack of sexual awareness.

No man wants to be repulsive to women so that behaviour just shows how a lack of experience and sexual awareness combined with a dose of arrogance creates these pigs and predators.

If you do have sexual awareness then you will give a woman one of the things that turns her on more than just about anything, undivided attention and appropriate behaviour.

If you are relaxed about sex you can focus on her and she may wish to talk or play or just do a million things apart from sex and you can enjoy each other in that way. If you do actually let a woman act naturally then generally speaking, she will talk herself out and become totally relaxed. There is a moment, almost to the exact sentence, when you have paid attention and really listened that a woman will finish with the talking and get with the action.

So, guys if you want to really impress the ladies, shut up, listen and really pay attention!

## Men we're not trying to be dirty bastards, it's just our nature

In this politically correct environment, there are a great deal of naive, ignorant and just plain stupid people who honestly believe they are going to somehow change the nature of Men, Women and the human race. Talk about self-delusionary arrogance – who do these people think they are and who do they think they are kidding?

A lot of big operators learnt years ago that it's best to humour these strange people and just keep on doing what they are doing rather than get involved in a load of nonsensical BS.

So, when you see the female panel show talking about how women won't be objectified, they then cut to an advertisement with a great looking chick hanging off anything from a new car to an air conditioning unit.

You see the ugly truth is that ratings set the ad rates and the ad rates pay those presenters and when the BS stops the station has to earn money and when they have to earn money, they have to run ads that work. Men are genetically designed to be obsessed with pussy - end of story. Car and pussy, boat and pussy, water pump and pussy.

Watch almost any movie and in the first 15 minutes the scene arrives where the leading lady enters the story. Hollywood call its "here comes the C", but I know you don't like that word ladies, so I will just say it's called "here comes the pussy" scene. We're not trying to be bastards that's just the way we are naturally. We like pussy, we want to fuck pussy, we want to look at pussy, we want to talk about pussy, we want to think about pussy and if you ever want to have a sane conversation with a man then you need to drain his balls so for a very short amount of time he can think about something else besides pussy.

Men produce 1500 sperm a second, because nature has put us here for a job. As soon as men empty their balls, they start to fill up again, and the longer the time between coming, the cruder and more aggressive they get. It's exactly the same thing that happens when we're really hungry which, as you know, is another primal instinct.

If you have ever been really hungry, you'll know your sense of smell becomes incredibly good, your focus unbelievable and your aggression intense. Eating and fucking keep the species alive and everything else is BS until those two needs are satisfied. Some people have no table manners and some men have no sex manners.

## Man does not live on bread alone

I think we've established that man needs pussy. That's why guys resent their girls, at a primal level, if the woman doesn't regularly have sex with them. The problem is that, if a woman doesn't fuck for their man because she is angry or resentful about something, then the animal side of man will hate the source of food (pussy) that won't feed him. Although this book is about sex and primal instincts, it's actually about getting a handle on sex so you can enjoy a great life focusing on all sorts of other things apart from primal instincts. Without the primal instincts satisfied though, humans can't fully focus on other things as much. Think about being really hungry and trying to focus on a meeting you are at for example.

## It's not about sex ...even though it's all about sex.

Sex is a wildly overrated part of our life and, in many cases it's just a damned nuisance too, but it's a primal need so we can't avoid it or ignore it and that's the ugly truth.

If you don't understand sex and learn how to manage it, then it can cause all sorts of heartbreaking problems like divorce, family break ups unhappy kids and sad lives all over one person engaging in the reproductive act at the wrong time with the wrong person. Everyone has the instinctive need to reproduce but we all practice different degrees of discipline and behaviour, just like we do with gambling, booze and drugs too. No matter how nicely you put it though, people have to fuck, and they will either get that urge out, one way or the other, or be angry – hence, I would suggest, the road rage and general anger shown in life these days. It's no secret that Hitler was sexually dysfunctional and look what he did to the world. Sexually satisfied people, generally speaking, are likely to be laughing and whistling rather than fighting.

So, sex is just a programmed primal itch that, once scratched, will be forgotten about till the next time the urge comes along. We are just vessels robotically obeying our DNA requirement to reproduce. The sexual urge is erratic, untrustworthy, fickle and often ugly.

Love, on the other hand, is steady, pure, consistent and a lifelong source of joy, if we're lucky enough to meet that special magical one who we can live with "happily ever after"

Sex can be many things including just a fuck. A man and a woman who don't know each other can be having sex in less than 3 minutes and that's got nothing to do with love. Lust too, is something that can be enjoyed but not trusted, it's fleeting and totally unreliable. You can base your life, society and all our future happiness on love, whereas sex, is only focused until one or both of you cum. It's insane to put love and sex in the same categories.

Remember when you found out when you were a kid that

your Mum and Dad actually did the "Dirty Deed" in order to create you. Most kids I was with at the time said, "No my Mum and Dad didn't do that". It seemed dirty and at dinner that night you would look across at those two deviates and think "I know what you've been up to"

I agree that kids shouldn't have to think or worry about sex when they are young because it's all ribbons and curls for the girls in particular and no mention of the fact that their Prince Charming will sooner or later want to cum in their mouth and have a 3 way with their best friend.

## Guys are attracted from the outside in – Women from the inside out

The tension between men and women arises because of their conflicting ways of looking at the opposite sex. A guy is attracted to a woman from the *outside in* and a woman is attracted to a man from the *inside out* because (in a primal sense) this guy may be the father to her children.

Just as women don't understand the primal nature of men, so too men don't understand the primal nature of women. A lot of men spend most of their life turning women off when all they need to do is shut up and understand the value of timing and the nature of the gentler sex.

Whenever I hear guys talk about woman, and how hard it is to get a fuck, I know they have no idea about women because women are actually dirtier and more sexual than men if you put them in the right environment. I am so confident about my ability to sleep with women that I am one of those few very lucky males who can actually get beyond that obsession about getting sex and really enjoy women as people.

That's the magic of understanding the primal needs of men

50

and women, because once you can do that, then you can really enjoy people because you don't worry about the sexual side of life.

As I mentioned before I know, within 30 seconds of meeting a woman, whether I am sexually compatible with her. If I am compatible, in nearly all cases I will never fuck her, but more importantly the ones I am not compatible with I can enjoy knowing, we'll never have that sort of relationship. I am a free man and can enjoy every person for who they are.

## The Dick can't fake it (or impotency isn't just a medical problem)

Every day there is some advertising about impotence in men and yet they never confront the problem in nearly all cases and that is … the dick doesn't lie. If a man does not feel like a man, to the woman he is trying to have sex with, then he is unlikely to get a boner. If he resents the woman, he's trying to have sex with, or feels humiliated, then it's not going to happen. That is also, I believe, part of the reason men start dating younger women. The younger women are more trusting happy and enthusiastic. I actually wonder, in a primal sense, that when a woman goes past the age of being able to reproduce whether she is genetically designed to be bitchy, so men are turned off and go to fertile women. I have met many beautiful older women, but I have also met some very repellent ones too

So, ladies, if you want your man to get a hard on, then don't blackmail him with sex, don't make him beg and instead be respectful and encouraging, as of course, he should be to you.

## The pussy doesn't lie

If you don't make a woman feel beautiful and desired, then

51

her body reacts the same way. I went out with a woman whose ex-husband bullied and manipulated her all through their marriage. They broke up and the first time we had sex she went into almost hysterical laughter which freaked me out a bit of course. She then pointed at the wet sheets and told me that all during her marriage she had a lubrication problem down there, and despite seeing various specialists, she was basically dry when her husband tried to have sex with her. I was really good to her, and her body reacted naturally, and even abundantly, in the lubrication area. At that moment, after years of anguish, she realised there was nothing wrong with her and it was a psychological problem with her husband.

So, if the woman you are with won't tell you what turns her on then how can you find out?

It's simple - the Pussy doesn't lie. If you start giving your girl scenarios as you're having sex with her, you'll find that her pussy instantly becomes wet naturally when you talk about something that turns her on or you do something that excites her. You don't even have to acknowledge that you know at the time you can just store that information and then do something with her later. Whatever you have physically done that turned her on you can explore that further later too.

Some of my girls have been turned on by playing with other girls, being used by multiple men, some by being submissive and humiliated and I give them what they want, and man do they love you for it.

If you've ever wondered why bastards get the nice girl's part of the reason is because bastards push the limits and say and do things that those sweet little girls can't suggest or do on their own. So that sweet little thing may look shocked at what you suggest yet in reality that's probably what she wants but is too shy to ask for. As the famous Yoda almost said, "Luke .... use the Pussy"

## Guys think sex is physical

Whenever I hear a guy or girl focusing too much on the physical side of sexuality, I know they have no idea about what's important.

No woman is going to take offence to a big dick, just as no man is going to take offence to a big set of breasts, but if you really believe that you can base your entire life on the physical side of a relationship then, quite frankly, you're fucked.

Even the technical act of humping and pumping is not very exciting by itself. Sexuality is eroticism, tension and enjoying the pure beauty and animal attraction of your partner.

Most women get bored with a guy who fucks forever, yet guys think it's great because they watch pornos of guys pumping for hours and think that's the way they should fuck. A lot of guys in pornos are gay actually, which is why they pump forever, and the shots are edited and crossed over including using stunt dicks so, just like a movie star doing amazing stunts, it's all special effects folks. Most men look at sex like a mechanical function of performance and often stress about how they are going compared to the pornos. That's like worrying about not being able to flip 10 times in a car, get shot at a hundred times and walk away without a scratch like the heroes in the movies do. It's not real life. Sometimes a long hard fuck is what the lady folk want but, it's about paying attention to the desires of the moment, rather than being an automated pumping machine. It's about the experience as much as the act. A great deal of the experience is how your partner feels after it's all over too. Make a woman feel beautiful and desired or make a guy feel strong and handsome and you will rarely be alone in your life.

When a woman thinks she can't get a man because her bum's too fat or her figure isn't great then it shows she doesn't understand men. All men want a slim waisted Big Titted Fucking Machine, just like you ladies probably wouldn't say no to the fireman in the calendars, but that BTFM (Big Titted Fucking Machine) or the fireman aren't going to last very long if they don't have anything else in common with you.

Having said that, if you do have let yourself go ladies or you're out of shape guys, I would have to ask why. Going back to the most important thing in life, which is to have a happy healthy relationship and family, why would you enter the race with a handicap?

I am amazed at how many people are single and looking for love but don't make the effort to look their best.

No man or woman can be unattractive unless they don't care about themselves. In fact, experience has shown me that really good-looking people are usually not as socially developed as regular folk, because they don't have to try as hard.

Regular men or women, who do not have traditional good looks, are usually the most fun if they are confident, happy and learn how to make people feel at ease.

A woman who is too keen and doesn't value herself because she is not classically beautiful actually shows that she doesn't understand her role, her sexuality or the power of herself as a woman.

A woman literally creates life within her body, and it all happens through her pussy, so the entire power of the human race is between her legs. Man has to get into her pussy, and she can command anything she wants when she gives the man who wants it hope.

## Men are always ready for sex whilst women need time

I would suspect the reason men are ready so fast and women take a lot longer is a primal need that relates to procreation. The male is probably horny and ready all the time because he only needs to pump for a while before he shoots his sperm and does his job. The female's body however probably has to get prepared to accept that sperm and be in the best condition to get pregnant. Instinctively therefore the woman will not be receptive to sexual advances as quickly.

## Guys be gentle first, and then a sexual animal if she wants that later

One of the biggest complaint's girls have about guys is that they try to get into it straight away because they think that women are like men. In fact, women can even get very wet and still not be in the mood believe it or not. You have to be gradual and gentle and not just focus on a girl's boobs and pussy because they pretty well view that as gross.

You will get there but first start with their mind and then caress their body gently excluding their boobs and pussy and talk to them and be appreciative of how they look and how they turn you on. They must turn you on or you wouldn't be trying to have sex with them so tell them about it, but not in a crude manner. Don't say "gee you've got nice tits". If they have a nice body tell them they really take care of their body and enjoy it. Appreciate those beautiful curves and stroke and gently run your hand across their body, be sensual not sexual. Paying attention and really focusing on the mood of your woman and creating a sensual environment is great when the time is right. Be a man and be strong and make her feel like a woman. Once you do start getting into it then you can be an absolute animal and screw the living daylights out of her if that's what she wants. So, my message is be a gentle starter and a dirty hard finisher.

## The hunting instinct of the cave man

Men are hunters and women the prey. Just walk down the street today and you will see women looking down so that the hunters (men) can look at them as they go by. The fact men are hunters is why it's nearly always men who attack women and not the other way around.

Thankfully most men can control their cave man urges and not go and attack and physically overcome a woman. Tragically some men display animal like behaviour and act in a way that is incomprehensible to normal people in modern society.

It's important to understand the hunting instinct of the man because if, as a woman, you pursue a man, in many cases you may not end up with him as you have basically taken his hunters role. There are many ways, as a woman, you can make it very easy for the man you want to hunt for you. Even the most basic things, such as lowering your eyes when he looks at you, shows a submissive act that the BDM, (Big Dumb Male), finds almost irresistible on a primal level. When it comes to the chase, ladies be submissive and don't worry, once you have them for a while, you'll get the influence you want. Once the mating ritual is over, traditionally the woman will run the show and that is a good thing because my experience has shown that women are far more sensible and capable in most areas of life. Sorry guys.

## When mating, women submit, and men dominate

Before you start getting insulted, just do me the benefit of the doubt and assume I love and respect women, which I do.

I am not saying women are inferior or shouldn't be paid as much or shouldn't have equal opportunities. Anyone who disagrees with equal rights is not sexist they are simply selfish, and selfish people use anything they can to push a cause that suits their selfish needs.

I am not talking about the outside world here either, I am talking about men and women at a primal level. If you don't understand your primal nature, then there is a good chance you will fuck up your relationships and pick the wrong person for you.

## The importance of appropriate behaviour

In the old south the plantation owners had workers specialise in different areas of the house, including having a kitchen wench and a bed wench. The lady plantation owners probably had a Field man and a Bed Man too. In our modern society that is not really acceptable, so as I quoted before, from the 1910 playwright "A lady in the parlour and a whore in bed" should also be extended to "a Gentleman in the Parlour and a wild animal in bed". In modern leadership terms this is called "adaptive leadership" where a leader adapts his or her leadership to the environment and situation. If everyone understood that, we wouldn't have people acting like animals in the Parlour instead of the Bedroom as happens quite often. It is incomprehensible that a Hollywood producer could be so out of sync with life that he would (allegedly) masturbate in public into a Pot Plant. He probably went home and acted like a gentleman in the bedroom too I suppose. If everyone applied their sexual behaviour to the correct environment, we wouldn't end up having men behaving like animals in the outside world because they would get it all out in the bedroom. The amazing thing is that we understand that socially. Few people, for example, swear or talk about sex in front of their grandmother or small children because they know that is inappropriate. It's the same thing with sexuality, and I will single out men here, if they adapt to their environment and act appropriately their life will instantly become a whole lot better. I am not saying this to boast, because this has nothing to do with me personally, however from an early age I learnt to behave appropriately, in a sexual manner, and my problem in life has been being offered too much sex not suffering through lack of it. More than once I have had to sit there and calmly explain to a beautiful woman why I shouldn't fuck her even though she wants me to. What she doesn't understand at the time is she feels that way because I have acted appropriately and given her what she wants at the time in many ways that are non-sexual. Guys, if you want to become close to a woman then shut up, pay attention, really listen and give her whatever she needs at the time. A hug, a warm drink on a cold day, a soft word, some gentle encouragement. Do that as a man and you will have a beautiful relationship with that woman. It may become sexual, it may not, but either way it will be beautiful.

## Achievement and sex drive are related

During the height of the depression, an author named Napoleon Hill worked in the Whitehouse for President Roosevelt and asked for one dollar a year as payment. It is said that Napoleon Hill wrote the lines "The only thing we have to fear is fear itself" for President Roosevelt. Mr Hill's job was to get the country back on track and, as part of that job, he wrote one of the most amazing books about achievement ever written. "Think and Grow Rich", which has now sold over 100 million copies, was the science of success using knowledge gained by interviewing leading figures of that era. The only chapter that seems out of place in this book is the one entitled *"The mystery of sexual transmutation"*. You can read the book, but in summary it states that sex drive and the drivers used to achieve a successful result in any undertaking are essentially one in the same. If you look at the traits of success and the activities a man, any man will go to in order to get sex then you will see what this book is talking about. You will realise all men have the seed of greatness in them – unfortunately though their focus is pumping that seed of greatness into the nearest available and willing woman.

Definition of purpose, focus, imagination, persistence, a never say die attitude, overcoming rejection, are all the traits you need to succeed get sex from a woman - think about that.

If a woman guides her man with her sexuality and makes him feel great, then that sexual drive can be used to create and produce a heck of a lot. Likewise, if a man does the same for a woman or a same sex couple do that for each other. Sexual drive, in its purest form, has massive power that should be guided and used in the right way, not suppressed and twisted.

# Love

*I* am a romantic by heart and I love that love is the consistent thread that makes life beautiful and creates healthy societies because love isn't an urge that, once satisfied, is something you lose interest in. Love and natural beauty, like a radiant sunset, a shimmering blue ocean, or an open fire give us a constant feeling of beauty and warmth.

We act far more naturally about love than we do about primal needs though. As you have probably worked out already, most of the world is made up of gentle, kind people who just want to live a peaceful life. Unfortunately, bullies run the world and so these people, and the powerful organisations they run, have learnt that the best way of manipulating people is through guilt and shame about primal needs. They know primal needs are unavoidable, so they wield power through them. Sex, Death and Love have been the staple of manipulating people since the beginning of time. Think about that.

The Beatles were right, all you need is love. Eternal, beautiful, magical and forever love.

I wish life was just one big romantic comedy movie, I really do, but the truth is that the human animal has been designed to survive, and in order to survive there are some basic primal needs that have to be taken care of like Food, Drink, Sleeping and Screwing .

The Food, Drink and Sleep part are taken for granted by most of us in our modern society, but the screwing part is something that most people are pretty messed up about.

There is so much BS, hypocrisy, nonsense, self-delusion, self-deception and manipulation in the area of sex that most people, and I am talking about the greater majority, are unbelievably naive when it comes to their sexuality and the sexual personality of their partner.

What's really interesting about sex, as one of the primal needs, is how twisted and obsessed society is with it, and that's only because we have been brought up that way. So many things have been attached to sex that have nothing to do with the actual act. A man and a woman can meet and be having sex in less than 3 minutes and that's a fact and that is why it's a basic primal act.

You also lose interest in sex, just like food and water as soon as you're satisfied so it's not reliable or trustworthy like love, which can last a lifetime. You can also fall in love someone who you do not suit sexually and still have a great life because sex is such a small part of our weekly activities.

## Could this person ever be your soul mate?

Forget all that B.S. about you having similar interests as your partner because it is simply not true. You do have to have the same values and beliefs about how to live your life and how you treat people and behave but that's about it. Forget about what they look like or what they do for a job just *focus on how you feel and behave when you are with them.* If that person makes you laugh, makes you feel comfortable, loved and you feel deep in your heart you can trust and care for them and they will do the same for you then that's the key. If they don't turn you on then maybe you can't be together, but the opposite often happens where people meet and are turned on by each other and confuse primal lust with a potential marriage partner, disaster. I've had sex with women I don't even like, and the sex has been incredible, but I don't confuse lust, tension and conflict with love so please, for the sake of your future happiness, don't do that.

## Ladies, I suggest avoiding one-night stands when you're single

Apart from your experimental stages and when you are happily settled with a loving partner, you are simply not designed to have sex with a whole lot of different men when you are single and emotionally available.

I talk a lot about lust but when you're single it's not about lust it's about love and every guy you sleep with will be one that there may be a glimmer of hope that something could grow from there.

You're vulnerable and available which means, whether you admit it or not, you will try to use your honeypot to attract the BDM's (Big Dumb Males) because it's in your DNA regardless of any BS you tell yourself. Instinctively you know that and it's amazing how all that BS stops when it has to, and females reveal that they understand the true nature of the game at its core.

I knew a guy who was a minder for a Rock Star and every girl who went near that Rock Star knew that acting all innocent and shocked at the fact guys wanted to have sex with them just didn't cut it in that environment. The result was they knew the deal was they gave their pussy to the boys as the price of entry into that world so they either chose to do it or they didn't. Maybe the guys were crass in that way, but the girls had the power to do exactly what suited them.

## Sexual faithfulness and love

Love is beautiful and ever since we were old enough to listen to stories, we have heard about the handsome prince fall for the beautiful princess and how they both live happily ever after – true love. I know that can happen and I believe that is the way life should be. Imagine if everyone was lucky enough to meet and be with their true love – imagine how happier and safer the world would be. Happy, content people usually don't start wars or cause that many dramas.

I wonder how many true loves are lost simply because people don't understand that a woman is naturally designed to share her romantic heart with, ideally only one man, whereas a woman's pussy is designed to have a lot of different men's sperms in her so she has the best chance of becoming pregnant and is impregnated by the strongest sperm.

Herein lies our problem in modern society with the concept of linking sexual faithfulness with being faithful in love. Ideally when someone gets married, they can be happy and content with that person forever. If they have shared values and they are kind to each other then there is no reason they can't be happy, so the problem often isn't about happiness in love. The problem is that one or both of the partners have primal sexual needs that aren't met. Everyone gets bored with the same sexual partner after a while but that doesn't mean they don't love their partner. Generally speaking, over time, love increases and lust decreases.

They may both be very happy but sexually frustrated (by the

desire for something new). In another version of the President Coolidge joke, there is a story about an older couple visiting a farm and the farmer points to the Bull and says "this Bull services these 50 cows" and the wife says to her husband "why can't you be like the Bull you don't even take care of me once a week" and he says "yeah but neither would the bull if he was screwing the same cow for 40 years in a row"

When a married man trying to chat up another woman says "my girl doesn't understand me" one would have to ask. Why would having this girl suck his dick make his girl understand him more. It's a load of BS and typical of the nonsense people talk about sex and relationships.

I have never heard a woman say, after sleeping with another man, "I just wanted to feel a different man inside me". They always have a million excuses that don't get to the essence of why she had sex with another guy. Women worry a lot about what other women think so they simply cannot be direct about a subject like this and perhaps they don't really understand themselves why they did it. Usually a woman sleeps with another guy because of her an innate carnal need to be desired by another man and to give a man she likes or desires pleasure. There's nothing wrong with that and it doesn't mean she doesn't love her husband it's just being desired and hunted by another man is exciting and after being together with the same partner for years the very nature of being together means the existing couple can't be that exciting. That's natural because old can't compete with new but that's Ok because that's just lust and lust comes (excuse the pun) and goes very quickly. Lust is immature, untrustworthy and unreliable, whereas true love is the opposite of all those things. That's why it's so important to separate the two and not destroy true love over lust.

## Be naturally sexual as much as you're able

Every couple wants intimacy and without doubt the horniest dirtiest sex you'll ever have in your life will be with a partner you totally trust and are therefore very intimate with. The physical side is only a small part of it. It's the freedom to be able to be sexually expressive in any (harmless) way you want. I have never been to a Hooker however I believe they provide a very important service for our society by ensuring horny men with limited behavioural ability are kept off the street. I also believe men go to Hookers partially because they can express their sexual desires without being judged and that's the problem with partners who are not prepared to do that.

Sexuality is a driving force so the person can either supress it, which is not healthy (unless it's something genuinely bad), they can find it somewhere else, which means they are going to be personal and intimate with someone else or they CAN express it with their own partner and have a deeper relationship.

As you have probably worked out by now, I am a highly sexual human being, yet I have never been to a Hooker, never been to a Swingers party and I only rarely have sex with other women who are usually ex-lovers of mine and with my wife's consent. The thing is though, that both my wife and I can do anything we want in private and with discretion. Just by knowing that we rarely do and would never endanger our relationship over something so trivial as sex.

I am sexually expressive because of my wild upbringing, "and you can't put the clown back in the box" as it were, so I can't unlearn all that I know about sexuality and nature of people and I need excitement and sexual expression. In my case I get that by arranging other guys to have sex with my girl once in a while because it's exciting and fun and she is such a sweet little thing it's our dirty little secret.

65

My girl enjoys it and she just view me as a little boy who is visual, like all males are really visual, so she just humours me and we both get a bit of a thrill. She is very easy to get along with for a week or two after her encounters I might add too.

Before I was married, I used to have wild times with a few guys and a girl, so I am used to doing that. Experience has shown me that the guys who have sex with a woman in a group sex environment will lose interest as soon as they come, so I don't feel threatened by them at all. I organise things in a way that ensures they can't get complicated either. I get guys from out of town, so they are gone the next day and they never know my girl's contact details either.

## Judge not – lest you shall be single and alone

There is no easy way of saying this. The more judgemental you are about sexuality the lonelier and harder your life is going to be, it's as simple as that. You may say "but I have a partner and it's all good", yet if you are judgemental sexually, there is a strong chance your partner is living a double life, either physically or in their imagination right now. We are sexual creatures and we need to express our sexuality. If it can't be honest and at home, then we'll simply find another outlet. Sex is a primal instinct, like eating, it's not something we can turn off and on, we can only direct the flow.

Look at our world right now and think about how much trouble is caused by people having sex with the wrong people at the wrong time. The broken marriages, the kids with their parents split up, the financial and social costs and a lot of time it's just "wrong dick in wrong pussy" stuff.

I am not promoting a sexual "free for all", but I am saying that the cost of misplaced sexuality in our world right now is crazy and it won't stop in the future either.

Never before in the history of the world have people been able to get a stray fuck so easily and so, with people's inherent need to express their sexuality, coupled with an instinctive desire for variety, people are only going to get more promiscuous as time goes by.

I believe the time has come to revaluate the way we view relationships and maybe create some socially acceptable rules around our new world of sexual freedom aimed at keeping marriages together and family units happy because isn't that more important than anything else?

I cannot tell you how many times people comment on how happy my wife and I are and how radiant and happy she looks. They ask us what our secret is. In our case we decided a long time ago that having a happy stable family life was more important than anything else and so, after finding out each other's sexual fantasies and desires, we played them out in the right way and the right environment.

In our case that means that my wife and I have had various sexual adventures over the years in a discrete and safe environment. We both like a bit of variety now and again and, as she has had a lot less experience than me, she has enjoyed a lot more sexual adventures than me. There's simply no way we'd let that interfere with our lives though, so those liaisons were very rare and always private, and no one has ever known a thing about them. As partners who have that sort of freedom, could you imagine us worrying about one of us leaving the other because of something sexual. The chances are zero. Of course when we first decided to do that we weren't sure how it would work, but we quickly learnt that sex is simply an animal act and the ironic thing is that one of the few times a woman can really enjoy casual sex is when she knows her husband is going to take her home straight after the guy has finished. Sounds strange to you I am sure, but the bottom line is we have a very relaxed honest marriage. It's not an "open marriage" as such because we don't socialise or ever flirt with other people in public. We only have private sexual adventures. We don't do anything with our friends, so they have no idea because we don't want those two worlds to ever meet.

If you can be honest and work out a way that you can have sex with the right person at the right time and not ruin your relationship, your marriage and consequently perhaps your kids stable upbringing then you will be amazed how relaxed and happy you can be about it all.

As a woman you may find some of your man's sexual desires strange but if you allow him to express them with you then he will remain incredibly close to you and also appreciate and respect you for being a real woman and understanding the primal nature of men. In short ladies, provided your man doesn't do something that is ethically wrong, just humour the bastard.

## Forget pick-up lines or fancy moves

Most people are scared of public speaking and using a pickup line to pick up a girl is possibly even worse than public speaking. It's also a skill like Roller Skating and the problem is guys with a good ability to pick up girls will get more girls than a quiet guy, but they may pick up girls who they are totally unsuited to. It's the same for girls who will go out with a guy that may be totally unsuited to her just because he's good with first impressions.

If you're a guy you need to understand that just because you can pick up girls, you shouldn't confuse that with finding someone you're suited to. If you're a girl, you should enjoy the fun and charisma of a good pick up artist, but you shouldn't confuse that with someone who would be a good life partner.

In truth pickup lines or any sort of short-term attributes (like good looks, good body, etc) can be enjoyed but not relied upon.

## Primal attraction – you should know in 30 seconds

Don't try to analyse attraction just be aware of it. You should know in less than 30 seconds whether you are sexually compatible and attractive to a person you meet. That doesn't mean you will ever have sex with them, but you will know and then you can know what sort of relationship you could have with that person. That means freedom because you can meet a beautiful looking person and know straight away that there's nothing there and then just enjoy that individual as a person and be their friend if they're a good person.

On the other hand, you may meet someone who is a bit of an arsehole but still have a strong sexual attraction and you may have sex with them a few times, but you will never be their friend.

Just be aware that sexual compatibility and partnership compatibility are two totally different and unrelated things

## Being liked and being attractive are different

If you want to learn about men just watch your dog. Have some food in your hand and that dog will totally focus on that food. The dog will sit up and beg, try to anticipate your every move and just be your best friend. Now replace food for Pussy and Dog for Man and there ya go.

Most men are desperate, like dogs, and they act like the current piece of food (Pussy) may be the last one they ever get so they're desperate and hungry for it. But most guys confuse attraction with being liked. When I was young, I was tall, not too hard to look at, pretty athletic and I'd always had a constant fuck since the age of 14 so I have never worried about where my next fuck will come from.

At an early age I learned that being liked by a woman and being attractive to a woman are not the same things and that's why when Men try to align with women they often fall into the "friend zone".

As a young guy though I couldn't care less whether a woman liked me or not and I let her know it. Unfortunately, guys are so "hungry for da pussy" that they will listen to any BS a woman speaks and never pull her up on it. Sadly, often good-looking women become crashing bores and are terrible in bed because they are humoured so much, I assume it's the same with good looking guys too.

Call me crazy but I think we should all aim to bring the best out in each other and I know when I start talking like a Wanker (and believe me I have and I do) then that lasts exactly as long as it takes for one of my mates to hear me and then it's all over because they let me know I am being a loudmouth Dickhead in very short order. Sure, it stings a bit but then I learn to behave better, and we all need that. People with money, fame or power rarely get contradicted and if they don't control themselves, they end up being boorish dicks. Caesar's slave whispered in his ear "you are only human", to keep him grounded.

## First be a primal mate then be a friend

The amount of absolute BS that is written about how to attract men is absolutely staggering and it's mainly because the articles are written by woman (because men don't care).

Women by nature are "aligners" and so when they talk to other women, they always look for common things they both like and they actually think that is important to men too.

These articles talk about having common interests but that's the icing not the cake so forget all that BS and focus on the core things and if they don't work then everything else doesn't matter.

Are you attracted to that person on a primal level? Do you feel they are attracted to you? Weird but strange observation. If the person you are interested goes to the toilet straight after you then that usually means they are interested in, you. It's like the dogs sniffing each other but on a more civilised level I suppose. I think it may be to do with primal compatibility but that's just a theory of mine based on no facts at all just so you know. Maybe you think I am mad but just take a look next time people meet and see for yourself.

## Men - Have a boy's heart below a man's head

The essence of this book is all about the right timing. Act the right way, at the right time, in the right place. Guys struggle with this and often act like immature jerks when they should act like grown men and women are always the ones who suffer. It's great to act like a boy in the right place but it is essential to act like a man in the right place too.

It doesn't matter how far we evolve in life women still have a much harder life than men. I'm not talking about washing the clothes or cooking the meals type hard I am talking about the harsh and aggressive nature of men generally. The raw male animal is, well, an animal and that animal is a predator and an aggressor. Very few men worry about women molesting them as they walk the streets at night. Very few men feel the pressure a woman does if a guy wants sex or just the girl to go out with him and she rejects him. The threats, the pressure, the bullying, the lying and the manipulation usually come from the male side and it's the woman who is scared and vulnerable. It's the woman that worries about men fighting, driving drunk or too fast and killing themselves or others through various aggressive or dangerous activities.

It's the men who start wars, rape and beat women, fight based on pride and generally cause most of the trouble on this earth. Basically, most men are arseholes to a certain extent, and I am a very easy-going person, but I still have that arsehole aggression lurking inside me.

Be a man when you should be a man and a boy when you should be a boy.

Woman do like the little boy in men and, as the old saying goes ,"when she sees the little boy in you, pretty soon the little boy will be in her", but women don't like or respect men who act like children in responsible areas when they are grown up. Without exception this causes huge amounts of stress and heartache to women and it's all because a child is actually living in a grown man's body.

There is a story about a researcher knocking on the door of a house and an 8-year-old boy answering the door wearing a huge, expensive dressing gown, holding a lit cigar with a glass of brandy in the other hand answers the door. The researcher asks, "is your mum or dad home" and the kid asks, "What do you think?"

Imagine if you let an 8-year-old boy drive a car, drink booze, take drugs, gamble and do anything to a girl. He would make himself sick through gluttony and abuse and leave a trail of destruction behind him. We've all met or know of people like this and, just like a child, they lie or try to blame someone else when they get caught. Society, the government, their parents, the boss, their partner or anyone else they can blame. Children make a mess and let everyone else clean up too because they are not old enough and grown up enough to be responsible. Some people never grow up inside. Sadly, it has been my observation that it is usually the male of the race that doesn't grow up because women have to grow up to become mothers.

If you want to give your woman a happy life, then show her the boy in you in the right environment and be a man when it counts. No woman likes or respects a guy who is an irresponsible jerk. They just put up with him because they don't have the energy to change, are too scared or they are not in a financial position to leave.

Consider the opposite. You drive carefully, pay the bills, abide by the law, contribute to society and then when you play you have fantastic wild fun. It may be sexual adventures, it may be thrill sports, it may be travel but whatever wild things you do you make sure they are done in the places where that's what it is meant to happen. If you give your woman an exciting happy life by being crazy at the right time and the right place, she'll be a very happy camper

## Women, money, protection and bling

It's a common belief that women go with men for money, but is it money or what money can give, which is security? Having a good provider and being able to pose a bit as well is not all bad. Right from when girls are very young, they love flashy sparkly stuff and as they get older that flashy sparkly stuff gets increasingly expensive.

So, if a woman had a choice of marrying the man she loves if he was broke or rich then she'd probably like him to be rich. In my case, I have been rich, and I have been poor and being rich gives you so much more freedom and will provide your girl with lots more sparkly stuff. It's funny though because being too rich or being too poor can make you very self-centred so a happy medium works pretty well. Money though is like wearing a top hat, you take it off and there's still the same person underneath, so if anyone marries just for money then they are setting themselves up for a pretty sad life.

When I was young my pals and I had no money, but we got beautiful women because we gave what they needed inside. We were hard bastards, but we did make them feel like women and if your woman feels loved like a woman respected like a woman and cared for as a woman then money is just the bonus deal.

## Women deserve to be protected

Although it's a long way from the Cave Man days, the female still instinctively needs to be protected by her man for both her and her children's sake, it's a basic instinct. I knew a married couple who got a divorce and I can remember exactly the moment when things started to change. The wife was getting picked on by her boss and was really upset about it. The husband tried to justify the boss's behaviour and didn't support his wife and that was the beginning of the end.

Forgetting about who was right or wrong, the wife felt threatened and needed to be protected and that was the bottom line. I am not saying the hubby should have fought the boss, but I am saying that the hubby should have done whatever it took to protect his wife. Whether it was her leaving work or him talking to the boss, he should have acted immediately. There is nothing more important than the primal instincts of love, warmth and protection. I didn't mention sex in their because it's just an animal act and you can't rely on short term desires. As soon as you're satisfied full you have absolutely no interest. Love, warmth and protection are consistent needs that can last a life, time sex lasts till the guys drops his load.

## A man's true nature is revealed after he's cum

That short period after a guy has cum is one of the few times in his life where he can actually be alive without that nagging need to have sex and that's why Hookers say guys talk and talk and talk after sex. Hookers offer two key services, sexual release and no judgement. If you can do that for your partner, you are most of the way there. When a guy has cum, he shows his true nature because he doesn't need or want for anything. If he is kind and considerate, he's a keeper. If he is selfish or dismissive and you don't feel good about yourself then that's how your life will be once he's gotten over the initial thrill of getting you, think about that.

## Sexuality versus core values

I am astounded in this day and age that people still list off traits in an ideal partner like it's a shopping list or a job interview and yet they don't even put on the list the "Givens" or "Deal Breakers" that will determine the future happiness of their lives. This is your life; this is about passion and lifelong love and it's not a logical process. Love is spiritual and emotional

The first thing is that the ideal partner must "give you the horn". You have to be turned on and really attracted to them. I am not talking about just sexually and chemically, but I am talking about values and behaviour too. Kindness, honesty, for-giveness are lifelong traits that can "give you the horn" long after your basic sex life becomes boring.

When I have sex with my girl I do it with so much passion be-cause she is a beautiful human being and I love giving her plea-sure. She is a an incredibly sexual woman with an amazing body but that, on its own, is meaningless. It's the honesty and genuine nature of her spirit that gives it to me.

75

There is not a guy my girl has had sex with that has not felt better and more confident about himself as a person and I love how she brings out the side of men that make them feel powerful and confident to be themselves. I really love that. I know it may sound strange talking about what traits I like in my woman as another guy is fucking her but if you haven't done then you don't really know what I am talking about.

The irony is that because we have freedom sexually sexuality takes a back seat to enduring and lasting values and traits as bizarre as that sounds

The other thing is to ensure that you or your partner is not sexually and spiritually frustrated all the time and you have to be realistic about that. If you're a woman who likes to get gang banged once in a while, then your partner needs to be cool with that and create a situation where you can do that safely and discreetly. If your male partner wants to have you and another girl once in a while, then you need to be comfortable with that. If you're not, then that's going to end in tears. There is no right or wrong here and no one should try to convince you otherwise, it's just what's right for you.

## People leave if they feel bad and sad

If you want to lose your partner in the fastest possible time just stop making them feel good about themselves and proud of themselves. Basic respect for each other as a male or female animal is an absolute must and when that respect goes it's the beginning of the end. I do mean manners and good behaviour but I also mean that you look up to your man if you're a woman and treat him as a man and if you're a guy you worship your woman and treat her as the most important part of your life and enjoy her as a sensual woman.

Many years ago, I read one of Bill Cosby's book and the way he described his wife and essentially how she was pretty cynical to him. I said to my wife I thought that the chances of him remaining faithful to her were about zero because men need to be respected by their woman and woman need to be respected by their men.

Men all over the world leave their wives for younger women but I would wonder how many leave their wives because they find a new woman who treats them like a man and makes them feel proud about themselves again.

In the play "Shirley Valentine" the star is talking about her husband and says, "he's not the man I married" and she thinks for a minute and says "but then again I am not the woman he married"

We all change over time and it's easy to become like growling bears at home and treat each other with a lack of respect and cynicism. Like everything else though, what's easy is usually bad for you and treating each other with disrespect is easy.

I have always been staggered by how rude people can be to each other in private and yet they treat perfect strangers with great respect. It's crazy when you think about it because the people you are close to are the only ones who really care about you, yet they are also the ones you can express your anger and frustrations on too. If you take away all the trappings of modern life, we haven't changed much in thousands of years. A man wants to feel like a man and a woman wants to feel like a woman. I believe one of the main reasons couples break up or play up is because they don't feel proud of themselves around their partner anymore.

## If your partners keep leaving you

Let's assume you're not an arsehole or childishly selfish or a liar or petty or jealous or mean or over critical, because if you are those things then you deserve to be alone.

Let's say you listen to your partner, you encourage them, you're thoughtful and kind but the dirty fuckers keep leaving you – why, why, why?

The answer is that you're picking the wrong partners. But why would you do that?

You do that because in most cases it's more natural to follow patterns that are comfortable to us rather than patterns that are good for us. We mistake ingrained habits with feeling "natural" or "right" about someone. Have you ever thought that your instincts and gut feeling about people may be wrong if you keep having your partners leave you?

There are few things more depressing in life than trying to change yourself and second guess your behaviour all the time and you don't need to do that.

If you have spent a long time getting repeatedly dumped, then try something totally different and stop focusing on the other person's qualities and attributes and instead pay attention to what traits they bring out in you. Are you relaxed, are you confident, do you feel your heart slightly rise when your partner says or does something, or do you feel your heart sink at some of the things they say or do?

I read a story about a young golfer who went to a golf pro and the golf pro told him he could play a lot better if he changed his whole stroke. When the golf pro showed him how to hold the club, he felt so contorted and unnatural he said "this is ridiculous it feels so unnatural" however he persisted and did get better.

A few months later the Golf Pro asked the young golfer to hold his club the old way he had done for years. Now when the young golfer went back to his old grip, he said "now this feels so unnatural". The Golf pro said "Don't confuse feeling natural with being used to old habits"

My point is that what you call feeling natural is probably just being used to old habits and those habits of choosing the wrong partner is why they keep leaving you. Forget about feeling natural or unnatural, they are probably just old habits.

## Overcoming the fear of your partner leaving you because of extra marital sex

I have confidence in the fact that if you are suited to a partner and, if you love them and take care of them, then they are unlikely to leave you. I think though when you really love someone there is always that hidden fear of losing your partner. I realised that the reason people often get emotionally involved with others during affairs is because of the nature of our society. It forces married people to be secretive in order to satisfy their desire to have variety in their sex life. So, the secrecy required to have alternative sex also includes intimacy outside of the partners and that can create problems in any marriage. As strange as this sounds, it has been my experience that playing up with your partner actually enhances your intimacy, whereas affairs diminish your intimacy as a couple. As I've mentioned before, a man and woman can have sex within a few minutes of meeting each other but it takes a long time to develop trust, love and intimacy which can last a lifetime. Sex is an animal act that needs to be managed within the context of creating and keeping a happy marriage. Hence a slight change to that old saying "A couple that strays together stays together".

# Don't change yourself change your world

If you have ever had someone say to you "you need to toughen up" "you think too much", "you can't live your life thinking it's a fairy-tale" or "you're too trusting" or a hundred other things that essentially say "you need to change" then here is one of the most valuable pieces of advice you may ever have in your life. Don't change who you are, just change the world you live in.

You are who you are, and you will only truly enjoy your life if you can act naturally. Now I am going to assume you are not a total arsehole so if you are continually told to act differently it simply means you are in the wrong environment for you. For example, if you work in the construction industry and you are sensitive then chances are, you'll find it hard. If, however you go and work as a volunteer at the local theatre on the weekend then you will find that your gentle nature is an asset.

If you are quiet by nature for example, then you shouldn't go out to nightclubs to meet a partner because that will be very hard for you.

Everyone has a natural confidence in something they do in their life, it may be cooking, writing, riding a bike, but whatever you do, that is the place you should be if at all possible, with the opposite sex so you can be yourself.

Even further than that, some people don't actually fit in with the culture and nature of the country they live in. In that case you should travel around and see what place does naturally fit who you are. Sooner or later you have to be yourself so don't change who you are just find the world you can live in naturally and your life will be changed forever. It's the same with sexuality, if you have certain desires and you don't hurt anyone then find a partner who is OK with that and get on with your life.

## To thine own self be true

Probably the expression that has caused more suffering in relationships than just about any other is, "do you know what the problem with you is". I would suggest the correct answer is, "yes I picked the wrong partner". Unless you're evil, a serial killer or just a horrible human being, what that person is saying is that you are not *exactly*" what they want. They are either reflecting their insecurities onto you or it shows an immaturity about the world and the fact it wasn't actually created for that person's sole benefit. Be yourself and If they are not happy then find someone who you make happy, it's as simple as that.

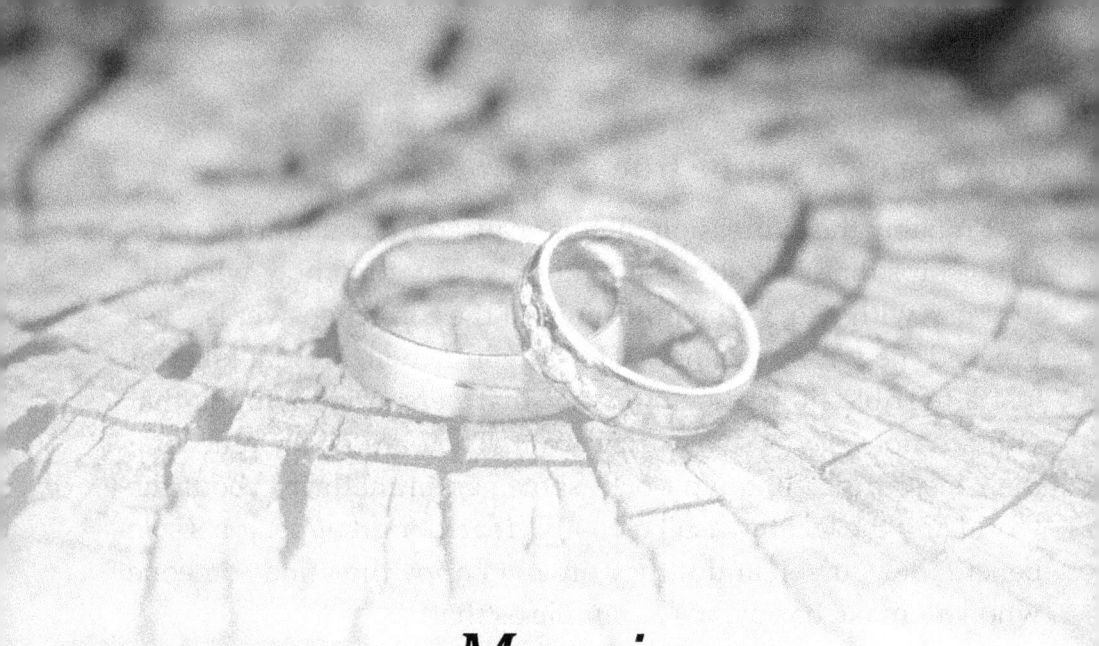

# *Marriage*

## Marriage Version 1.0 (launch date 2350 BC)

*M*any years ago, in a place far, far, away, marriage was "invented" by some very wise people to ensure the land and wealth they owned stayed in their family. It wasn't even religious originally. Today it's about love and creating a safe and happy unit to bring children up in. In those days people looked at sex, marriage and love in a very different way and that's the difference between happiness and misery – the way you look at things. There were village tribes for example where every full moon the villagers would drink, dance and then take any partner they wanted home and go for it. The next morning everyone woke up, went back to their partners and never mentioned it again. If we got brought up with that as being the normal thing to do, we wouldn't think another thing about it. Apart from being physically or mentally cruel to people, everything else that happens to us is only good or bad because of the way we have been conditioned to think about it.

In today's society so many marriages break up and there are

so many broken homes that it makes me wonder how many people could have stayed together if they had just focused on keeping together a happy family unit as their number one priority and then adjusted their sexual and social behaviour around that with dignity and respect for their partner. If you both expressed your desires in a private way in consent and without disrespecting your partner, then things can work. In our society we simply haven't accepted that. Instead we continually see perfectly good people end up expressing the need for sexual change by sleeping with someone from work or a friend and often ruining a whole lot of lives in the process. Often all that drama is caused over the primal need for sexual variety and the primal need to be desired by another mate.

I am not advocating total sexual freedom or open marriages, however I am just asking you to consider, that if we lightened up about sexuality, how many marriages could be saved and how many kids could be living in a stable two parent environment instead of being involved in single parent households, break ups and divorces.

It's amazing that no one will admit our old system of marriage and a lifelong sexual partner rarely works these days. People just keep getting married and often play up and then get divorced and I suppose that's because they just don't know what else to do.

In my case my wife and I have been happily married for a really long time and the chances of us breaking up over infidelity are absolutely zero; simply because we manage that variety side of our lives in a different way.

Now, before you have images of us going to Swingers Clubs and wearing dog collars, I can tell you we've never been to a swinger's club. That environment would be just as strange to us as it probably would be to you, so that's not the way we live our life. I have never even been to a prostitute in my life. It's not because I have anything against them, but simply because I have always been able to get as much sex as I want. That's because sex is not as important to me, compared with other values and traits, and women can sense that in a man.

In our case we decided that the most important thing in our lives was to bring our kids up in a happy and stable environment and sexuality was a trivial, animalistic urge that needed to be managed privately and in a way that could never threaten our marriage.

Most people, whether they admit it or not, are terrified of sex and their partner's sexuality so they live a double sexual life either in their mind or in reality. That's sad because they lose an intimate side of each other and if they can't express that side of their lives then that part of their life will take up more time in their mind that it needs to.

Like anyone who has a great deal of experience in an area of expertise I am very confident about sexuality and don't take sex too seriously at all. I keep it very much in perspective.

Sex, like food, is something you can become obsessive about when you don't get fed regularly.

The result of my "unusual" and pretty interesting sexual life is that I have no fear of sex and I know that it is a trivial and largely irrelevant part of life, unless you're not able to express yourself sexually, then it's a big deal.

Once you understand and are completely comfortable with sex then the real values in life are free to come through.

If you wish to be free of the fear of sex, then you need to remove your lack of knowledge around sex and sexuality.

## It's all about love

Years after the fairly comprehensive sexual education I experienced, as a young guy, my now wife and I decided to get married. We decided that happiness, and a stable family environment for our children, was more important than anything else, including the usual attitudes about Love, Sex and Marriage.

In fact, I would say that more nonsense and misinformation has been written about Love, Sex and Marriage than just about any other area in life and that is probably why half of all marriages end in divorce. Think about how you would rate your level of expertise about any subject where you were provided with no proper education, misinformation and your practical knowledge came from purely random experiences. That's our standard preparation for marriage. How would you expect to rate your ability on a scale of 1-10 ?

In any other area of life there would be a major rethink about the way we did things if the failure rate was half of all attempts. Imagine if pilots learnt to fly on the same training schedule as our sex and marriage education. If every second plane that took off crashed, people would not tolerate that. I believe we tolerate a 50% divorce rate because we don't know what else to do.

When you consider that the single biggest force of destruction in our society is broken marriages and relationships then surely it's worth having a fresh clean look at the way marriages and relationships work and doing whatever works that is legal, fair and within reason.

## Why do so many marriages end in tears?

The first and most simple answer to that is the same reason we become unhappy about anything.

Unhappiness is created when there is a difference between what we *expect to happen* and *what actually happens.*

In the case of marriage, each person at the altar has a set of expectations and then, somewhere in the relationship, these expectations are not met to the point of becoming unbearable and that's the end.

I am not saying all marriages fail because of sexuality in some form or another, I am saying that a lot do fail because of everything that is associated with sexuality in the marriage vows that were created centuries ago.

We live in a world today where there is an abundance of variety in almost every area of life. Our attention spans are probably shorter than they have ever been and our ability to access whatever we want through the internet is almost unlimited. We can travel the world and enjoy different cultures and people very easily.

The amazing thing though is, that we have regressed with our outlook on marriage because marriages were far more liberal centuries ago. Men and women could have multiple wives/husbands and they even made allowance for extra marital affairs in terms of property claims.

I wonder how many marriages would have stayed together these days if we had a more liberal outlook?

So, getting back to our expectations on marriage, we now have two people at the alter who are almost certainly sexually experienced with each other and probably others too. In today's world, they will always have access to an abundance of sexual variety too. The newly married couple are expected to walk out of the church and never have any variety in the sexual side of their life ever again. Do you feel that is a realistic expectation? Do you think that may be a big contributing factor as to why over 50% of marriages fail? If sex with the same person becomes boring, then that leads to sexual inactivity, which leads to frustration, which leads to anger, which leads to fights and therefore differences and arguments will become more intense and aggressive.

Now I am sure you are thinking right now that there are many other factors involved in marriage break ups and of course you're right. But which comes first, the chicken or the egg?

## The danger of secret sexual affairs

When someone satisfies their sexual primal need for variety, under the current accepted rules of marriage, they have to be secretive, so they have to become intimate with their new sexual partner. That secrecy will bring the new couple closer together, whilst at the same time, making the person having the affair more distant from their existing partner. So, the secret side of the new sexual activity creates intimacy possibly more through secrecy than sexuality.

My wife and I have had sexual encounters in a discrete environment and known nothing about the other couples because we have separated everything except the sex part so there was maximum lust with minimum intimacy. That way there was no chance of either us ever becoming close because we never communicate and work together with anyone else in order to be secretive.

## Ladies, I know you think he's not like that, but he is exactly like that

I'm not a marriage therapist so I am not going to try to understand other reasons why marriages fail but I am going to relate, through my own practical experiences, about how to not let sexuality interfere with a happy marriage. In order to do that, the first thing you need to know is the truth about men and sexuality. As I mentioned before, you will probably say, "my guy is not like that", and that is the problem. He is like that. I think it was Confucius who said, "the character of man is different, but the nature of man is the same". As comedian Billy Crystal said, (in the movie Harry Met Sally), "A guy wants to sleep with every pretty woman he meets". Meg Ryan asked, "what about the ones that aren't pretty", to which Bill Crystal replied, "they pretty well want to nail them too".

## Givers and Takers

Here's a simple philosophy on life. If everybody got this, the world would be a much better place.   When you're a kid you take, when you grow up you give. It's that simple.

The problem is that there are a lot of immature people who don't seem to understand that and spend the rest of their lives being kids in adult's bodies. These spoilt brats often convince those around them who are kind to them that somehow there is something wrong with the kind person and the giver.

You know the scenario. The guy plays up, lies and then he says things like "it's no big deal" and is all cool about it. The thing about these people are they are always cool at someone else's expense.

It's the Bullshit that arseholes use to play on the forgiving nature of others and the inherent slight self-doubt all normal, sincere honest people have. As Rudyard Kipling said in the Poem **IF**. *"If you can trust yourself when all men doubt you but make allowance for their doubting too"*. The only people who don't have self-doubt are unaware dumbos who spend their life wafting around in "an ignorant air of self-importance".

They are bad company because they make people feel bad about themselves, and often attract women not based on building those women up but on keeping them down, and that's a road to lifelong misery. "Treat them mean and keep them keen" is great fun in the college years because the ladies like a hard man, however if you want lifelong happiness and a happy marriage, find someone who "treats you great and keeps you (happy) forever".

## Have the same level of sexual awareness

Sexual awareness isn't about the act of sex, it is about how much emphasis you naturally have about sex. There some people who look like they have never had sex in their lives, and they go on to invent the splitting of the atom and provide dam good dental work. (apologies to all you sexy dentists out there). There are other people who almost ooze sexuality out of their bodies. Neither of those traits are right or wrong, it's just nature giving life a balance. If you have a high-level of sexual awareness then you are the kind of person who could be in the emergency meeting room talking about the nukes that are coming towards your city right now and still, in the back of your mind, think "wow that person is hot". It's pathetic but true. If both of you are like that, or neither of you are like that, then that is OK. If one of you views the world through people's sexuality and one doesn't then there is a whole world one of you is unaware of and can't really share with the other and that's not so good. A person with high sexuality won't be too shocked if their partner wants sexual variety but someone with low sexual awareness may be stunned and shocked by that and make the other person feel guilty and ashamed which is just wrong. You shouldn't feel ashamed with your partner about your natural sexuality. If you are, then you have the wrong partner because you can't really live your life as yourself. The exception to that of course is illegal or immoral activities that hurt others. Sexual awareness is different to your sexual personality because some people have a highly sexed personality but just can't handle it. These people are pretty fucked up and spend their life in denial, or guilt if they do something sexual. Hypocrites in the media and life are usually people with a highly sexed personality but they are not aware of their sexuality. They are the ones who condemn everyone else for having affairs and then eventually get caught out themselves.

## Marriage, Sex and Hollywood

Hollywood has a lot to answer for as far as confusion about love, sex and marriage goes. A great example is Ralph Fiennes. In the movies he often plays a wonderful romantic leading man and yet in real life he took a Qantas stewardess he'd just met and fucked the living daylights out of her in an airplane toilet. The sad part is she told everyone about that because, everyone has both the romantic leading man or woman and the raw sexual animal in them, and if he wasn't a Hollywood star no one would have known.

When you think about it, it's pretty frightening that Hollywood, probably the worst example on earth of marriage, relationships and individual stability, is actually showing us how to have a good relationship. That's probably why the movies end as soon as the characters get together because the good folk of Hollywood have no idea what people in real life really do after that.

Love happens very quickly and easily in the movies and Hollywood almost always relates love to sex, but that's total BS. Being gentle and sweet at a romantic dinner is beautiful but fucking a girl like that becomes very boring very quickly. Don't kid yourself, once in the mood, women like to fuck like wild animals and any woman who says otherwise is kidding you and herself.

Having sex with someone you love is fantastic of course but, in a primal sense, your body will get bored pretty quickly with the same partner because we are genetically designed for variety. The problem is that we destroy marriages and families and the happiness of kids on a regular basis just because we've got bored with our regular fuck.

I am not saying that we should all become sex maniacs and hedonistic, who just fuck whoever we want whenever we want, because most of us don't do that with our other primal needs such as food, drink and sleep. Overindulgence in almost anything is generally not good for you, and it's just the same for sex.

## The changing nature of marriage during the course of history

The challenge is that the model we have now for marriage is not working that well and many people become bored when it comes to their primal sexual needs, hence the millions of married people on sex dating sites. Our view on sex is a cultural thing too. In some societies the men used to fuck every potential bride to see how they were suited before marriage. In other cultures, multiple partners were acceptable so it's just what you are led to believe is ok, not the acts themselves.

Up to the 16th Century it was common to have sex with other people around because poor people shared rooms. Even the Royals had servants in their Bed Chamber 24/7. The Wedding march – "Here comes the bride" relates to when the bride and groom were walked to the bedchamber by their parents and church members. Everyone came in the bedroom and a curtain was then drawn so they could consummate the marriage. Meanwhile the family and priests played cards in the bedchamber. Talk about pressure

## Sexual variety is the Elephant in the modern bed chamber

Today we have regressed and our whole society is in denial about sex in marriage. It's the massive marriage destroying elephant in the room. I mean don't you think it's amazing that it appears no one has ever left their partner because they got bored fucking the same person for 20 years. We all know that everyone gets bored with that, no matter how much they love someone. There's nothing wrong with that and it doesn't mean you don't love your partner. That boredom is about lust, not love, and "you can't trust lust". Love on the other hand is eternal. When I hear advice to wives about dressing in new lingerie to excite their man, I can't believe how sexually naïve these people are and so out of touch with the male and female animal. If you want to excite your man do a 3 way with another woman or ask your hubby if he wants to see you picked up by another man and that will excite him, but a new pair of matching bra and knickers, I mean, please.

## If you don't explore your partners sexuality, chances are someone else will

Maybe your girl has fantasised about trying it up the butt for 20 years and then one night at the Christmas Party a guy tells her he wants to do that to her. She may fake surprise, but he has planted that exciting seed in her head and eventually that usually means he will be planting his seed in her bum. I am not trying to be rude, but men or women who bring up a sexual fantasy someone else has held in their mind, can have an unusual influence on their life. It often happens to innocent couples who don't have the experience to put their sexuality into perspective so they can ruin their lives over an unsatisfied sexual fantasy.

# All men are bastards – here's why

When I was young, I had a dog and if that dog did something bad, I would call him and then punish him. Guess what happened after a while? That's right, the dog stopped coming when I called him. He had trusted me when I called him but when he came over, he got a belting.

I don't punish dogs anymore when they make themselves vulnerable to trust me and now, they will come when I call.

Men are in the same category as dogs. If you invite them to be honest and then beat them up, guess what? They are not going to be honest with you anymore. The challenge with women is that they are "aligners' and they want people to agree with them and think and act like them by aligning together. They can't understand men's piggish behaviour, so they are disgusted and upset by it.

If you as a woman, stop trying to align or understand a man's behaviour and just accept him for what he is (including behaviour you can't understand and don't like) without judgement you won't spend many nights alone. I can understand why you see men as pigs but if you want to have them confide in you and trust you then you can't plead for information and then hammer them when you find the man's actions unpalatable.

# A little bit of friction between men and women is perfectly healthy

There is nothing wrong with a natural friction between Men and Women.

Most women think that men are disgusting at times, because they are, and most men think women are temperamental nutbags at times, because they are.

The weakness for women is they want men to have the same morals and behaviour as them and that's where the problems start. Men don't think that way. In fact, primal behaviour is before thinking even comes into the picture. If men were not judged and free to do it, they would fuck every woman they met that they found attractive and even a few they didn't like. It's the male animal's reproductive job to insert as much semen in as many women as he possibly can. I am not saying that all men do that in our modern society, because we have separated ourselves from the animals by learning self-control, however all men are animals at a primal level.

Now if you are a woman reading this book and you go and ask your husband if what I have said is true, he will tell you it isn't. He will deny what I have said because he's scared of getting punished. It is true. If you don't believe me get him on a lie detector and see how he goes. It goes back to that mantra, "other men do that, but my man isn't like that". He is and if he denies it, he's lying to you. Don't punish him for it though.

## Happy parents create happy children

In an ideal world, everyone would meet one partner, mate for life and live happily ever after. How much happier would the world be if that happened? I'm not into the blame game, but at the end of the day, when parents split up kids suffer. When couples split up a lot of people suffer. Even though divorce is a common part of life these days, it doesn't make it good. I can't guarantee that this book will save your marriage but I can guarantee that, if you are suited to each other spiritually, then the sexual side of your life will never cause your marriage to fail if you use the advice that is relevant to you in this book.

In our experience we have enjoyed a really happy marriage and family by reviewing our existing views on tradition, convention, ego, pride and what we were taught to believe was "morality". Essentially, we were willing to try just about anything to give our marriage and family a better chance of staying together.

## Talk is cheap at the altar

I am always amazed at people who find out their partner have been playing up and they just break up immediately. The first sign of drama, pressure or indiscretion and they are out the door. Is that really true love? If you really love someone it should mean that you would put up with pretty well anything and still love them. That's why it's so important to be with your soul mate, someone who you truly love and who has the same spirit and soul as you. Someone who can really understand how you feel deep down inside without you even having to say anything. If you are with the right person then they will do things that make your heart rise up and feel elated. If you're with the wrong person you will feel your heart sink at some of the things they do. Think about those seemingly insignificant moments that you'll never forget. The ones that either broke your heart a little, or that made you look at that person and see how good they were.

## Sexuality should never ruin a happy family

If you have a happy loving partnership and a happy loving family, then there should be nothing more important than that. Not your pride, not your ego, not petty jealousy, because love, unlike lust and other trivial behaviours, can be forever.

What I see in the world today though is so many people ruining their families because they simply don't understand the sexual nature of people and, specifically, the sexual personality of their partner,

It's incredible how the same thing happens over and over

again and yet people seem to be surprised. Someone plays up, the marriage breaks up then kids are in a broken home. All that misery over a new fuck that becomes intimate because the couple have to hide and be secret.

I know that in order to have a happy stable family unit everyone needs to trust and respect each other so if my girl played up behind my back I would be just as devastated as the next guy.

We have accepted the reality and sexual nature of humans though. We have created a set of rules, as a consenting adult couple, that allows us to retain our respect and trust whilst at the same time expressing our primal sexual instincts in the right environment.

## Timing and sexual behaviour

We understand the need to do the right things at the right time in other parts of our lives. A man is prosecuted if he speeds down the street in his car but cheered if he drives as fast as he can on the racetrack. Yelling in the library is inappropriate but at a football match it's part of the game.

So, if you hold your family and partner above all else then you would do what needed to be done to ensure that all the needs were catered for in the right place. Need for speed on the racetrack, need to yell at the footy and need for sexual adventure in the bedroom where no one will see you.

Whilst we occasionally enjoy short term sexual adventures with other people, if a man touched my wife or approached her in public, I would be just the same as any other guy and deem that inappropriate behaviour and stop it immediately. Likewise, I would never show any attraction to another woman in public. In fact, we are probably straighter than most couples in public and in front of our friends and family. If you met us you simply would not believe that two sweet, happy people could be such dirty bastards in private. We have total respect and trust in our life and we also enjoy the thrill of knowing we sometimes enjoy a brief fling in our private life too.

## Ladies, don't let your man's sexual frustration ruin a happy marriage

I have to admit ladies that, men are so dumb and so primal when it comes to sex, it's frightening. That's why you should never let sex interfere with a happy marriage. If your hubby gets frustrated because he doesn't cum enough just basically learn to milk him like a cow, as disgusting as that sounds. Pull him off, suck him off, let him have sex with you, pose in front of him as he masturbates, but let him get the cum that makes him crazy get out of his body. As I mentioned earlier, men produce 1500 sperm per second, and they are programmed to use that sperm for pro-creation. The longer the sperm stays inside them, the angrier and more aggressive they become. Sperm has a shelf life and the male animal has to get rid of it in a certain amount of time. In a matter of minutes, you will go from dealing with an animalistic pig to a quiet easy-going person who just wants to go to sleep- it's so easy.

In truth, if you don't want to do that it's because you resent him. Withholding sexual pleasure is a powerful way to display your anger and resentment. If you don't believe me then try keeping him satisfied for 2 weeks and see what happens to your life. He'll do anything for you and follow you around like a puppy dog. The alternative is the male animal gets angry and resentful if their source of relief and animalistic urges has denied them. They will punish you in some way for sure just like you punish them by withholding "the goods" as it were.

For every action there is an equal and opposite reaction –

think about that.

## Men, take care of your wife's need as a sexual woman

Men are very mechanical by nature and, when it comes to sex, we simply need a bit of friction and to pump up and down a bit until we come. We are a pathetic, crude instrument when you think about it, sorry ladies. Sex for women is a totally different thing and the main difference is that women need to be in the mood and built up to it rather than just making it a mechanical process. Making a woman orgasm compared to a man is far more complex. I haven't done any research here so I am not claiming that this is a scientific fact, but my theory is that a woman is being prepared to make a baby so she must be in the right frame of mind to do that. Regardless of how sophisticated we think we are; we are still primal creatures designed to ensure the survival of the species. Whilst women need to be prepared and, in the mood, guys just have to be around with a lot of sperm anytime they are needed. Guys are like a 7/11 for sperm – open all hours and willing to serve.

So, if you want to help your woman have an orgasm then first start with her mind and her mood and then get onto the physical side later. A lot of women can't come during sex and that doesn't really matter so much either. If you learn to be good at oral sex or using your fingers (most men are too clumsy for this) then there are ways to give her a good orgasm and enjoy being there together.

Women are far more powerful and can easily take half a dozen guys in one sex session , as I mentioned before, so make sure you let her know that if she wants to use a vibrator or dildo that you are cool with that and she can use it alone or with you.

As hard as it is for you, as a guy, don't think mechanical, think mind body and spirit.

## Ladies don't break the sexual flow

If you disturb a wild animal when they are eating or priming up the opposite sex for a fuck then there is a good chance that you will be attacked, and it's exactly the same with humans. Look at fights in places where the opposite sex mingles and most times it will because another animal has disturbed the ritual of sexual advancement.

My point is that, no matter how long you have been with your partner, make sure you avoid the habit of breaking the rhythm of the build up to sex. If you start putting conditions on sex, or you stop the flow by not agreeing to do one thing or another, or you change the subject then you will be breaking the flow of the build-up to sex. Not only will that make your partner angry and resentful, but it will, on the male side, eventually make them impotent too.

Sexuality is so primal that, even if you are having a lot of other issues, then the chances are males will still try to have sex. So even if you have a lot of communication problems in other areas the one area that there will still be an attempt to communicate is while the male is trying to get a fuck.

The trouble starts when the female is (understandably) frustrated about the lack of communication in other areas. Sex is a powerful trading tool so if she stops having sex or uses sex as a bargaining tool then that frustrates and angers the male.

Whilst withholding sex from a male causes anger, using sex as a positive motivator can have great results.

So, if, as a woman, you make it clear that you need to talk about X Y and Z before the man gets to have sex with you then it will be a huge incentive for the male to talk about those things and sort them out.

Once you agree you are happy with that area then you must let the other partner go completely and become sexual with no hidden agenda or conditions.

If you're a woman you should be your man's sex toy and just do anything he wants even if you think he's a pig and an animal. If he wants you to bend over, put your head down and wiggle your butt while he calls you a dirty slut then just let him. Don't try to understand him, just give the baby his bottle. He won't mind if you're humouring him, or if you don't want to do it (in fact it makes a man feel strong when his woman is obeying him in the bedroom even when she doesn't really want to)

## Guys, bring her sexual personality out and she'll love you for it

I think the biggest mistake men make in the bedroom is they confuse the sweet little partner they are with every day with the sexual personality of their woman in private.

If the most important thing in your life is to keep your girl happy and to stay with you then you should be the outlet for all her sexual desires within the privacy of your relationship. If you do that, then she will feel loved and be free sexually and spiritually. She will also be uninhibited (and therefore not frustrated sexually). I am not talking about physical sexual frustration, because that's easy to fix, I am talking about erotic sexuality which we all have.

Guys if you have a sweet little girl who looks like butter wouldn't melt in her mouth, I can assure you that inside of her mind is an erotic wild sexual animal that she will never talk about or reveal. In fact, the only time she will admit it is the minute or so before she comes as she is fingering herself late at night and imagining guys gang banging her or licking cum off other women's boobs or whatever.

The weird thing though is that even though those fantasies are about sex, it's not about sex it's about the freedom to express yourself.

Why do people have certain sexual fantasies – who knows? But as long as it's legal and it doesn't hurt anyone, why are people so twisted and fucked up about expressing them.

Think about that for a minute.

You have a partner who you have sex within the privacy of your own home, and no one sees what you do. What is the difference if you create a private safe environment where your partner can express his or her sexual and erotic desires?

If having a happy and stable partnership and family is your number one desire in your life, then let me ask you this.

If you and your partner both live out your sexual fantasies together in a private environment honestly and in a trusting manner, which couple do you feel are more likely to stray behind their partners back. The ones who do that, or the ones who don't?

Over 70% of married men have been to prostitutes, why? Could it be because prostitutes allow them to live out their fantasies without judgement? Do you think your partner would be incredibly excited at living out their fantasies free of any deception or hurt?

I can promise you that if you have sexual adventures, discreetly, together and with clear rules you will experience a freedom and intimacy that will create a rock-solid bond between the two of you.

The challenge for both of you is understand and accept each other's sexual fantasies and, provided they are legal, and they won't hurt you then try them.

It's easy to find your partner's fantasies out too. As you're fucking your partner just create a few scenarios and if your woman's pussy goes instantly super wet you've hit the jackpot or if your guy's dick goes super hard then same for him.

The funny thing is that it is the men are often the ones who find this challenging because most men are boys who have never grown up. Women are very, very erotic creatures and if you put them in the right mood, they will essentially try anything.

Like ai said before, if you have ever seen a sweet girl with a real animal chances are that's because he satisfies her unspoken carnal and emotional needs. As a rule of thumb, the sweeter the girl the dirtier they are.

## Don't be a handbrake

A handbrake is someone who slows you down and stops you doing your best.

If you belittle your partner's dreams and desires in any area of life, sexual or otherwise, you are slowly destroying your life and theirs. Everyone, high and low achievers, have many plans and desires that they never bring to fruition. That doesn't mean they can't dream. Some dreams and fantasies are just that and they will never come true. Whether it is a sexual fantasy or a life fantasy, don't immediately judge your partner or tell them all the problems they would have if they tried to do that. Just let them dream and think. Freedom of thought is just as bigger a turn on as freedom of action.

All I am suggesting is you ask your partner to tell you about their dream rather than you are telling them why they can't achieve their dream.

I had a friend of mine who tried to stop smoking for over 20 years. Every few months he would tell me about the new method he was using to stop smoking. Every time I would listen and encourage him along the way. For over 20 years he failed, and for over twenty years I listened without knocking the schemes. It wouldn't have mattered how long he tried I would have encouraged and listened to every idea. After 20 years he tried something, and it worked. None of his friends made fun of his continual attempts at trying to give up and I am sure that is the reason he kept going. Don't be a handbrake that slows your partner down, let them cruise along down life's highway because you'll never know where it takes them.

## Ladies, Cynicism is poison to the heart of men

Men are simple creatures and a lot weaker than women. Keep them well fed sexually, literally and psychologically and they'll be happy. Humour their crude animal instincts and don't make them feel ashamed of themselves. Instead you should pat them on the head and tell them how good they are sometimes and make sure they feel proud of themselves then you will keep them for life.

The guaranteed way to have a man leave you, resent you or play up on you is to be cynical.

Every woman can be beautiful if she takes care of herself spiritually, mentally and physically. No woman or man can be attractive when they are cynical towards their partner.

*Cynicism is disappointment expressed in an ugly way* and it has the same effect on relationships as the iceberg had on the Titanic, it's going to result in a disaster. Ok let's assume you have been disappointed because your expectations haven't matched your life, welcome to the world.

In fact, having set expectations in an ever-changing world creates all sorts of problems. You can set expectations about you and your partner's behaviour and values because you can control them internally. You can't expect everything to work out exactly as you wished once you come into contact with the outside world though.

My experience has been that people who continually tell their partners what's wrong with them are reflecting their disappointment in their own lives. If things aren't working out the way they wanted then no one is stopping them from acting, why is it their partners responsibility?

Every man has to be looked up to by his woman, just like every woman needs to feel desired and loved by her man. If you feel your partner "has to earn your respect and love", well this is the chicken and the egg story. If you do faithfully care for your partner in these ways, then the man will be proud of himself when he feels like a king in his own castle. A woman will feel great being his princess. It sounds corny but in certain ways your romantic life should be like a fairy tale and, whilst you may not be the handsome prince and the beautiful princess you were when you first met, you should still treat each other that way every day.

If you're a guy you need to protect love and trust your woman and you have to make her feel beautiful and let her know she is the most important person in your life.

If you are a woman then you need to make your man feel like Prince Charming. I have said it before, but I wonder how many men leave their wife for a younger woman simply because they gain their self-respect and feel like a hero again. Men are simple weak creatures, don't forget that.

## True love, ego and respect

Everyone says, "Life is Short" and it's really true. If you find someone you love and care for then you are well on your way to having a happy life. Whether you realise it or not, when you find someone you love there is always a little fear in the back of your head that you will lose them. Sometimes both of you are going to muck up and it may involve another dick or pussy in that mess up. If you don't accept the possibility that this could happen then it may happen with someone you know or who is close to you. If that happens then you are creating all sorts of complications and respect issues that can last a long time after the event, embarrass you and often destroy your life together.

That's why it's important to never embarrass your partner. You can actually have sex with someone else in a private environment while your partner is there and not have any problems with respect at all. Just because one of you is going to have sex with someone else that has nothing to do with disrespect. Everyone can be well mannered and respectful and still be naked and fucking their brains out. Discretion, like in all areas of your private life, is the key.

## Tension and Release

Our life is made up of tension and release and if you have ever wondered why bastards and hard women attract the opposite sex then that's one of the reasons. You watch a movie and you know the hero won't get killed or that he'll get the girl in the end but you're still tense right up until the resolution and then there's the release. It's the same whether you go on a scary ride at an amusement park or you have an orgasm, it's all about tension and release. The stronger the build-up of tension the stronger the release - that's just the way it goes.

But if you're a happy easy-going person does that mean you

have to change and play games to attract someone? No, you should always be yourself however if you're aware of how things work then you are in a better position to choose how to handle any situation. It's like if you learn to be a good animal handler it doesn't change your personality it just helps you not to be bitten and in the case of dealing with the opposite sex not to be burnt by them.

So how do you create tension and release naturally? For girls, don't fuck on the first date because you haven't built up the tension and anticipation. Hope is more exciting than a fuck on a first date. Be encouraging and give him hope and he will hunt you like a hungry dog. No matter how much the guy likes you he won't value you as much as when he's had time to anticipate, work and enjoy his conquest. He's a hunter by nature so let him hunt and work for his dinner because if you don't you are depriving him of one of his primal needs, to hunt and conquer. Humour the Cave man in him and he'll love and appreciate you for it. Forget the BS they tell you in woman's mags about the modern woman who can chase men. Nothing has changed since the beginning of time and nothing ever will. These days we have flashy cars, houses and gadgets but, when it gets down to the primal stuff, the man still mounts the woman and fucks her just like they did in the cave man days. Dick fucks Pussy is primal, no matter how you dress it up

Ladies if you give the guy hope, he won't go anywhere. If you're a woman who worries about your man running away it's because you don't understand the primal nature of men. Forget everything else, primal attraction is where you have to appeal to him in the mating game.

If the guy doesn't chase you then, as the famous line says, "he's just not that into you", and if you start with that little interest from him, you'll just feel bad about yourself. Being unwanted will usually make you want the guy more because of how bad you feel about yourself but that will lead to disaster.

The best time to get out of there is at the start before you get involved with the wrong person.

It's the same for guys too. Girls do love being pursued by the man of their choice, however if they are not attracted to you at a primal level, then don't waste your time. Move on, because even if you do get her, she may stay with you and be secretly unhappy.

## Mutual interests don't attract partners, primal attraction and your scent does

When I read articles about crazy ways to attract a partner, such as learning their interests or getting good at the sports they like, I don't know whether the writers are just making fun of their readers or that they really have no idea themselves. Going into a new environment will expose you to new people, but it will still come down to animal attraction.

The focus for men and women is primal attraction first possibly followed by love. Values and interests are usually after that. That is why criminals and abusers get a partner in the first place I suppose. As a primal animal, you are not looking for a best friend, you are looking for a suitable mate to breed with.

Scientists agree that human pheromone (human body odour) influences sexual attraction. It stands to reason that we have to ensure, at a reproductive level, that the other animal we mate with is compatible with us in terms of producing a healthy offspring. Charles Darwin, the famous English Biologist, reasoned that our immune system gave off either an aroma that attracted or repulsed the opposite sex. What I am suggesting then is to expose yourself to different groups and let nature take its course rather than trying to do or be something you're not.

## Marriage with one true love and a variety of dicks

If you have been lucky enough to find your one true love and married him then that's beautiful. As I mentioned before, it's been my experience that women are not suited to share their heart around.

Every guy reading this would have had a girl say to them "I was hurt when I was younger". That's because young women enjoy childhood watching princes and fairy tales and then they enter the world and some bastard lies to them to get sex and breaks their heart. I hate pathetic arseholes like that. It makes the world sadder and can make women cynical too. They were so open and innocent and were abused for that. Women are not suited to change the person they love. They have to give too much of themselves each time and it's just not what they are made to do.

As the ones who have to bring up our next generation, I believe women are designed to meet that one mate and then have a steady environment to bring up the kids. Consequently, women are naturally romantic and search for that one lifelong true love, it's beautiful and I love that. Any woman who has found her lifelong true love is invariably a very happy, natural woman. The Yin and Yan conflict comes because on the other hand women are naturally designed to enjoy quite a few different men sexually in their life because their body enjoys and even craves variety, in a sexual sense, but not necessarily a spiritual one.

Unfortunately, women are not prepared for the sexuality part of their life when they go out and start dating and they simply don't understand the sexual side of men and what drives men. Hence the "bad experience when they were younger". They become aware of sex, like they become aware of Father Christmas and the Easter Bunny, but they never become aware of sexuality or their own sexual personality. At a primal level, all men are the same. They have to inject the female with sperm in order to keep

108

the human race going. It's the survival of the species programming that is still operating at the cave man level.

At a primal level, women are all the same, they need as much sperm as they can get, ideally from the strongest animals in the herd. That is why women get fired up by big biceps, tight bums and six pack stomachs on men. It shows the men are strong and therefore the offspring will be strong. They say women are also attracted to men with money. That is understandable, because with money comes power and the ability to protect the woman and her offspring, and that stirs the primal instinct of what's best for the kids. The conflict in marriage then is the desire for a steady love partner but the biological need for a variety of sexual partners.

If you deny or ignore your sexuality then, at best, you will become frustrated or bored with your partner in a sexual sense. If you are lucky enough to have a low sex drive, then you can probably easily live with one partner and never have any sexual variety and truly live happily ever after. If you have a high level of sexual energy, then the chances are you'll end up expressing it somewhere. If it's at the wrong place at the wrong time, then it may ruin your marriage and your family unit. Even if you are not caught, it will still divide your focus and damage your love bond with your partner. The choice is to accept your nature and then work with your partner on a solution that is honest, open with them and discrete, as far as the rest of the world is concerned.

## The powerful influence of women in marriage

I think we have established that men are a lot weaker, mentally and resilience wise, than women. It's not fair but that's the way it is. Even in today's modern society, most women still choose the full-time job of bringing up kids even when they have a career. They essentially have two careers for many years of their life. The man therefore still has a major influence on the career success of the family. Consequently, women do have a massive influence on their man's success and often their family's wellbeing. The saying "Behind every great man is a great woman" (and vice versa) is not just an expression. There's an old story that goes like this ...

A woman had a choice of two men to marry. The man she chose to marry went well in his career and eventually became the Mayor. When coming home from a formal function one night, her husband saw his wife's other choice of partner working on a construction site. He said to his wife, "Just think, if you married him you would have been the wife of a construction worker". His wife replied, "No if I married him, he would have been the Mayor"

Take a look through history and if you want to know what made a man successful don't ask him, ask his wife or his mother. From Einstein to Richard Branson, wives and mothers who encourage their kids and tell them the sky's the limit, create extraordinary men with extraordinary confidence.

As kids, they will believe anything their mothers tell them. As adults, men are tuned to raise their efforts and respect for themselves when praised and encouraged by a good woman. If you have never practised bringing the best out in your man, then you are not using one of the most valuable tools available to you. If you appreciate him, respect him and continually talk and focus on what you want him to achieve then the results will be amazing. If you don't respect him and you focus on his shortcomings, then that is the sort of performance and behaviour you can expect from him.

## A good fuck and a good marriage partner are two very different things

The problem with all the BS spoken and written about how sex and love are the same is that it makes people choose the wrong life partners for themselves. You may laugh at that, however as half of all marriages fail, that has to mean that every second person makes the wrong choice of partner.

Having sex with someone you love is awesome, but you don't need to love someone to have sex. You don't need to have sex to love someone either, so the two are actually different activities.

Picking a good marriage partner is basic animal attraction *combined with* common values, respect and admiration for the heart and soul of the other person. Having a good fuck is based on sexual compatibility.

Many people you may be sexually attracted to could be hopeless partners for you and you need to understand the difference between the two.

When my wife and I go out and have a sexual adventure it is based on physical attraction. We don't want to meet people who we may be spiritually attracted to. We are happy to have a play for a few hours, but we don't want to start a relationship with these people. Ideally, we aim for people who are totally unsuited to us in a non-physical way.

## Your partner is not a "one size fits all" and can't give you everything you need

One of the most dangerous threats to a happy marriage is the myth that your partner should somehow be your universal "fit every situation" person, that is total BS.

If you suit each other in terms of values, kindness and spirituality, however the sex side doesn't work that well, that's not the end of the world or your relationship. To add spice to your sex life you may choose, as we do, to include some "celebrity guests" once in a blue moon or you can do something else that works for you. It doesn't matter how much you love your partner; you are biologically programmed to get sexually bored with the same partner after around 18 months. (I'm not sure of the time but you can look up Google if you want to know exactly, I never said I was a scientist!)

So, if you base your marriage on raw sexual attraction, but your values and beliefs aren't the same, then you're well and truly fucked even before you start.

If you're young, then by all means be lustful and just enjoy that raw sexuality but for fucks sake marry someone you admire for their kind heart or generous nature, not the size of their biceps, bank account, boobs or dick. If you choose by that sort of criteria, I can promise you it will end in tears. Unless of course you and your partner are not deep thinkers and you judge things on a superficial level. That's OK, as long as you have aligned values in that area, because that's what will make or break you.

## Why men lie to women

Most people take the path of least resistance in life, hence everyone telling you that your clothes, hairstyle, dinner "is great". There are two huge motivators for men to take the path of least resistance when it comes to women. The first and foremost reason is, pretty well everything men do with their female partner, is aimed at ensuring they get a fuck. It's that simple. The second reason is because men are disgusting pigs by nature and ladies, at the risk of stealing a line from a Few Good Men, "You can't handle the truth".

Both men and women seem to be programmed to be naive and gullible in their own special way when it comes to the opposite sex. Men are incapable of understanding that they are not actually that special to a sweet-talking woman who is somehow making money out of them. Hence men saying, and believing, "No, that hooker, stripper, sales lady *really* liked me"

Women simply cannot handle the truth about the nature of men. Hence women saying and believing maybe all other men are sexual animals but, "*my guy* is not like that". It's unbelievable how naive and gullible both sexes are in these areas.

Men are disgusting to women in a large part because they have not been honestly prepared for the sexual side of men. It's all fairy tale stories with noble princes which I think is great however the problem is that girls get brought up with stories about dressing up and going to balls and yet, in reality, when they grow up, they dress up, go out and end up sucking balls.

The only men who aren't animals are the ones who have had their balls cut off, because the fuller their balls are, the cruder they become. They have to unload that sperm into a female to propagate the human race. Women have the same instincts too and if they don't get dick, they crave it so much that they'll find a dildo or anything else hard and "dick like" to fuck. That is just natural primal behaviour.

The fact that we have those primal behaviours is, in itself, not bad because they can be satisfied in the appropriate environment. The challenge is that women have never been told the truth about the raw sexual nature of men. The truthful side of men's sexuality is so ugly that it is a shock and almost impossible to come to terms with. That is quite understandable.

I don't lie, because I believe my character is the sum total of every action I take and every word I speak. I will not compromise my integrity for anyone or for any price. Boy has that got me into trouble over the years!

I cannot tell you the number of times I have been with a group of people where the girls have been calling me every name under the sun and yet I was the only honest guy in the group when talking about male sexuality. I would never discuss it unless asked, but if asked I would tell the truth.

I have been at events where nearly every married guy in the group had played up at some stage and they would be innocently standing there with their wives denying every word of truth I spoke. I could have proved my point and shattered every woman's dream right there by telling them what their hubbies had been doing whilst they were away on trips for example. I would never be indiscrete though, regardless of whether it was an indiscretion that a woman or a man committed. I don't believe I have the right to create drama without knowing the full story about the situation nor do I believe it is my position to do so.

Intimacy comes through honesty and when men live double lives in relation to their sexuality then they are naturally distancing themselves from their partners. When I looked at those wives and husbands, I felt sad that those women weren't being given the respect of knowing the truth.

The alternative to deception is to discuss your sexuality together in a non-judgemental way and see If you can fulfil each other's needs and desires in a private environment. The problem is if one of you does discuss it and you get humiliated or condemned then that could ruin your relationship. If your partner has strange or illegal needs that you cannot accept then you will need to make some big decisions. In most cases though, most fantasies aren't too harmful or radical.

If you do handle the sexual side of your life together you will find your partner will have little or no desire to do anything outside your world. If you can both enjoy guilt free lust and eroticism every once in a while, in an environment that is harmless and discrete, you will be amazed how relaxed it will make you feel in your life. The other funny side effect that happens is it allows you to focus a lot more on really important things like love, romance and achievements.

My girl and I live that way and the funny offshoot of that is that I am very conservative in public and with other men. I have never engaged the services of a prostitute or been a pig at a strip club or done anything inappropriate simply because I have enjoyed all my adventures privately and with my girl, so I am not frustrated in a fantasising sense.

We feel very secure in our relationship because my girl would tell me if she fancied a guy and I would tell her if I wanted to have an adventure with a girl I met. We have never done that because the only time we have sexual adventures is with people we don't know in our social circle.

So, men lie to women because they take the path of least resistance and they don't want to be punished for their true nature and they learn to hide that natural behaviour early on.

Sexuality influences women and controls men and, if you learn how to manage your partners sexuality, you'll be free to enjoy all the other wonderful things about them

## The one reason for anger

All anger and unhappiness come from the difference between what you expected to happen compared to what actually happened.

The bigger the gap the bigger the misery and you stop being

unhappy or angry once you adjust to the new expectation.

Most people go into marriage believing the fairy-tale and expecting to be super happy and excited with their partner forever. You can be happy with your partner forever but if you expect to be excited by the same person all the time then you are ignoring the fundamental desire of people for newness and change

Sex is an animal act and whilst it may be great to do it with someone you love it's not necessary. If you observe that, agree with it and accept it then the difference between the how you expect people to act sexually and how they actually act will change and you won't be angry about it anymore.

## Now you've got sex sorted, you can enjoy the really important parts of life

Throughout this book I have talked about sex, primal instincts, animal attraction and animal behaviour. It's all been pretty crude, basic stuff, but there is no other way to convey this information. Through my personal experiences I can promise you that, once you accept the sexual nature of man and woman for what it is, and then deal with it together privately, it will allow you to move on and focus on the more important values in life. So, by handling sexuality, you can actually spend far less time thinking and being distracted by sexuality.

The last part of this book talks about how we organise our private sexual affairs so that are safe, harmless and have no ongoing ramifications in our life. Whether you choose to actually do anything is up to you, but I hope this book has helped you become more relaxed and confident about you and your partners sexuality. I wish you all the love, peace and beauty that the world can give you.

# How To Experience Discrete Sexual Adventures

## Keep it private, just like your sex life is now

*I*n a normal sexual relationship, no one sees you having sex, so you are used to being discrete and guarding your privacy. You can do the exact same thing if you bring a bit of variety into your sex life.

In our case, we design our sexual adventures to be just like dreams. When we wake up the next morning there is no sign that anything has happened and it's just a memory. That means always use condoms for health, always meet in a safe place, I suggest a good hotel, never make a permanent record, using video or photos, and don't provide your normal email or phone number.

If you take those precautions, you will never mix sexuality with other things like respect, trust and intimacy. Even if you do something that you don't like, you can just leave and never talk about it or do it again. Bad sexual experiences are just like going to a bad restaurant, you get out of there as quickly as possible and never go back there again.

Not all our sexual adventures have been positive, but they have all been safe and we finished with them the moment we left the room.

## Never mix your sex life with your social life

If you go back through your life you will be amazed to see that the clothes you wore and the things you did can look embarrassing now. I think everyone goes through some, "what was I thinking" moments, and your sex life is the same. The great thing about having good friends and family is that they know you well. The equally bad side is that they can recall all the embarrassing periods in your life too.

The problem is, that you can be labelled for an action and then you must live with that forever. Your sex life is the same, and I am sure you have known someone who ended up sleeping with their best friend's partner, a neighbour or someone at work and then everyone found out.

One of the reasons we questioned the whole concept of a monogamous marriage was that every couple we knew, who had married when they were very young, broke up. In nearly all cases it was through an indiscrete affair or sexual experience because they had not been with other partners. The couples were always embarrassed because of the public scandal and the relationship was never the same. A lot of those couples had a good chance of staying together if they had the knowledge and experience to separate their desire for variety from their everyday marriage. A lot of people got hurt through their actions, kids, family and friends and yet the couples were good people.

## Planning sexual adventures at the right place and at the right time

In a purely sexual sense, a guy and girl can have sex, and as soon as the guy pulls out, the fuck is over. That all changes though if there is anything that happens to "freeze frame" the moment. If someone has sex with their partner's best friend, a neighbour or someone at work, there is a good chance people will find out and then the couple involved will be exposed and have to live with that forever.

They have had sex at the wrong place and the wrong time. But why do people risk their entire family and future over a stray sexual encounter? The momentary pleasure seems to be wildly out of proportion compared with the problems it causes to couples, families and our society.

The answer is, we are primal animals programmed to procreate and keep the species alive. We are also programmed to spread the seed around and have variety so that there is less inbreeding. This programming comes way before logical thought and reason. It is an animal instinct, like the need for food or sleep. We are taught to eat and sleep at the right place and the right time however our education about sexual behaviour is universally bad.

Our whole upbringing is filled with mixed messages, hypocrisy, guilt and poor or wrong information about sexuality in general and certainly about sex within a marriage.

It is therefore understandable that most people don't want to admit or confront the fact that they biologically crave variety. If you crave variety, at a primal level, that either means you can satisfy it occasionally or you must live your life in denial and suppress your natural instincts. If you never talk about it with your partner, then it will probably become a bigger and bigger thought in your head over time. As time goes by, and you become sexually bored with your partner, which you will, no matter how much you love them, then the idea will get stronger still. Now if you go somewhere and you combine booze and opportunity, then that is often when both the defences and the pants come down. Unplanned, indiscrete encounters like these are what ruin relationships, trust and often families. All because our society has made us feel so guilty about admitting our natural urges that we are afraid of discussing them and then managing them in a realistic and discrete way.

If you are lucky enough to have a low sex drive, then none of this will be a problem for you. If you have a high level of sexual desire, then planning to have discrete sexual encounters at the right place and the right time will change your life for the better in a huge way.

## Religion, Morality, Lust and Confusion

Religion and our strange and often hypocritical moral code have resulted in nearly every woman I have ever met being conflicted and feeling guilty about their sexuality. If you add to that, immature men who are indiscrete and essentially punish a woman if she does have sex with him, then is it any wonder women fear being honest about their sexuality. It has been my experience that nearly all women don't understand or won't acknowledge their sexuality and it is confronting for them. That's why when a woman sleeps with a guy casually there is always a justification. They had too much to drink, they were upset because they'd just broke up with another guy, they felt sorry for the guy, and so it goes on. It is never that they just got horny and wanted to fuck a new man. If you want your wife or partner to try something with other people, then you need to promise them that you will never judge them or use what they have done against them, no matter what happens.

You'll need to be patient too and you need to pay attention to what your partner actually wants. There is a thin line between sexual variety and just pushing your own one-sided agenda. If for example, you're a guy who just wants threesomes with another girl, that's probably all about you rather than working with your partner, so both of you can enjoy some discrete sexual variety.

## Sexual flings don't have to embarrass your partner

Guilt, anger, fear and betrayal have nothing to do with sex. If you carefully organise a sexual adventure, then you can both enjoy the pure lust and excitement of the moment. It is not going to mess up your marriage and, in my experience, it just builds a stronger bond between the two of you. If your partner however fucks someone and everyone finds out, then it's not about sex it's about respect, pride and embarrassment. The damage comes from people outside your relationship. If either of you play up and everybody finds out, then it makes life harder and sadder. Even if your partner forgives you, they will still trust you less and feel humiliated. That will weaken the bond you have together. The opposite is true if you organise a fling. You have planned it together, enjoyed it together and you are both empowered because you are treated with respect and told the truth.

It's also your little secret, and you can look at each other across the room and think about the dirty horny things you have done together, it's all very exciting for you both as a couple.

## The fear of Jealousy

It's natural to be worried that your partner could instantly fall in love with a new partner in this scenario, but it just doesn't happen. These events are organised just for sex and there is no opportunity to make it anything else. Even if it is great sex, it's

121

all over once everyone comes. Richard Branson talked in one of his books about wife swapping in his first marriage. He made the mistake of doing what we are making you promise not to do. He wife swapped with one of his best friends and his wife ended up leaving him for his best friend. Richard was young and naïve, by his own admission, because he did exactly what you shouldn't do and mixed his social life with sexual variety. Letting his wife have sex with another man wasn't the problem. It was letting his wife be with someone of similar values that messed up their marriage. My experience has shown that people leave an old partner for a new lover normally because it's a new person with new stories and, by virtue of them needing to hide, they end up becoming intimate. If it's' just "Wham Bam thank you Mam" then there is simply no chance to get intimate.

## Sexual adventures won't fix existing problems in your marriage

If you love your partner and like to see them have a good time, then this is just another way of you both enjoying something together. If you take the approach that it is an exciting night out once in a blue moon where you can go to new places, meet new people and then fuck them, then that's cool. If you do this to try to repair a marriage or add something that's not there, that's just not going to work.

## Choose a sex partner purely on lust

I have mentioned this before, but it's important to make sure the partners you meet are wildly incompatible, in a social sense, but highly compatible in a physical sense. My wife likes big tall boys with muscles, what woman doesn't? I am cool with that, but I'll make sure they have nothing in common with her at an intellectual level. That way I don't worry about her having fun with a toy boy occasionally. I like tall, dark, european women, and if they can barely speak English, I don't mind at all. We just want to spend a night with partners who are light, fun and socially incompatible

## Ensure you only have polite, discrete communication

If we do get a regular partner, and trust them enough, then we will give them my phone number after a year or two. Women are never a problem and we never give guys my wife's phone number because guys can get too keen at times. If the guys communicate with me, they are always respectful and careful because I am the gate keeper, as such. Our rules are very strict about communication. All text and phone messages are written with zero sexual content. So, if someone wants to meet, they just send a text "I'm coming to town and wondered if you're free for a catch up". As no texts, pictures or calls have any sexual content, it doesn't matter who reads or hears them. That ensures we never let any sexual adventure become tangled up with any part of our regular daily life. It's all about walking out of that room and returning to your normal life without leaving a permanent record.

## Be straight with your social circle

No one in our social circle has any idea of our sexual adventures. In fact, we never discuss any sort of sexuality with our friends. We want our friends for life, and we don't want to mix up short term lust with long term friendships. I think the fact that we get all our sexual side out in private is why we are so straight in public.

## Choose a safe environment and non-local partners

We usually choose people from interstate who stay in nice hotels in the city. Interstate visitors don't come to town too much and a good hotel ensures it's a safe environment. It also removes the risk of liking the experience too much and having that person try to chase you up all the time. If they live interstate, they can't just arrange a quickie anytime they want. Unless I have known these people for a long time (over a year at least), I will only provide a private email address made up just for that purpose. I will check the email once in a while, but they can't ring or bother us in our normal life.

## Don't commit to more than once

Any time we communicate with a new sexual partner we say it is a "one off" and that we do this sort of thing very rarely. That way if the first experience is not good then we just politely say that we won't be doing anything again like that for months and maybe years. In our case, we lead a busy life and it can often be months between adventures anyway, but it's just a polite way of not hurting someone's feelings.

## Use sex hook up sites

We use sites like Adult Friend Finder or Fbuddy because you can review the people on the sites and see what others think of the people you are looking at. There are a lot of immature men out there and cautious women, so it takes a bit of time to find nice discrete people. If you create a regular conversion (anonymous over an email you have set up just for this) you will find that they can't hide their personality and nature for very long and you can choose a good person or couple. Ladies are (quite rightly) distrustful of men on these sites and there are fake ladies' postings too. Even if it is a woman looking for a guy you would be amazed how long it takes sometimes to find a nice guy who is respectful well-mannered and thoughtful.

## How long it takes to set up dates

We are very careful, and we often go months without finding anyone who sounds suitable for a sexual adventure. I organise things and would only go on the website once a week most times for a quick look. I use the private email set up for this and never put face shots or details that would reveal who we are. I don't lie on our profiles but a lot of people (men) do. Remember that you don't want someone socially compatible, you are looking for people who are sexually compatible. My wife for example is a mature responsible woman, so if we find a guy 15 years younger than her, fit, single, and travelling interstate for work he could be perfect. He will want an NSA, (No Strings Attached), fuck and that's what she wants from him too. Likewise, if a mum with two young kids at home and no husband just needs sex once in a while then I would be happy to be her "beckon call boy".

I don't know why but, as a rule of thumb, we have found that the best talkers online are the worst at sex, so don't worry about their literacy skills, just focus on animal attraction and ensure that they are decent people who actually listen to what you want.

## How often we see people

We have a couple of interstate people that we have been seeing for over a decade and we may see them 2-3 times a year. On average I would say we would meet someone new maybe twice a year, because it's a very small part of our lives. You don't need to do this very often each year to really spice up your sex life. If you do try this, you may be super keen at the start, however after a while, you'll calm down and probably see other people once every six to eight weeks. Adventures like this are like everything else, if you over do it then it loses the magic.

## Don't create hook ups based on only one partners desires

Both be honest about your fantasies and try to organise meet ups that will suit both of you, provided your partner is cool with that. Ladies, if your hubby just wants another girl to join you all the time then that's probably not about you, as a couple, it's just about him. If you want that too then that's great, but if not, maybe you can take him to the hookers one night and watch him play with two girls if you don't want to get involved. He will be thankful forever if you do and it won't hurt a bit. I have never met a woman yet who has not enjoyed having multiple male partners in the right circumstances. I am not saying that to be provocative, it's just been my experience in life. Ask your wife if she masturbates and fantasises about being fucked by a group of big strong men and I can almost guarantee she has. If you want to let her try that fantasy then the best thing to do is find a good guy who you get to know and trust and have him organise a night with friends, he trusts. Take your time, we did that once but only after knowing the first guy for a number of years, so we were confident that his friends were trustworthy and discrete.

## Men, make sure she feels beautiful and desirable

It is a given that men are easy fucks and, in truth, so are women provided the timing is right and provided they feel good about themselves. My experience has been that I can get a woman to do just about anything my dirty mind can think of, provided, and this is not negotiable, that she feels great about herself. So, make sure you give her time to get a bikini wax and her hair done before playing around because she will absolutely insist on being waxed and well presented. Remember that this is primal stuff and she will be preening herself for a new mate just like you may have lost weight and gone to the gym when you had break ups in your life. We males are simpletons in this area, but it is a deal breaker for a woman so take it seriously and make sure she feels beautiful and desirable.

## Set the rules and agree on them before meeting

You need to have the other people involved aware of the rules and agree to them prior to meeting. We ask for absolute discretion from the people we meet to ensure that we stay in the moment and nothing can come back to haunt us. We will never go anywhere that has any chance of being unsafe and we will always be there together. Even though it is a sexual situation, we expect good manners and respect for each other. If someone doesn't feel comfortable, we make it clear that any of us can call it a night at any time. These things to me are not negotiable and once in a while guys, yes, it's always the guys, will try to ignore them. I bring some extra condoms because I have had guys turn up without them, which I find amazing. It goes without saying that this is the first and last sexual encounter they will have with us because that single action has shown they are inconsiderate people.

## Lighten up about Sex

I read a book about Christine Keeler who was the young girl that got involved in a British scandal with politicians in the nineteen sixties. She had sex with some major political figures and her pussy basically brought the government down. During that time, she went to the stately homes of major politicians and powerful businesspeople and enjoyed beautiful dinners with these dignitaries. She was amazed that, after dinner, these prominent people would all get naked and screw each other's husbands and wives' just as casually as if they were having dessert and coffee. She found it quite strange at first but then discovered that, in a discrete environment, it was amazing how much fun and relaxing a bit of naked messing around can be. Apart from anything else, I have found that women lose all their nervousness around a man they have had sex with. There is something incredibly liberating for a woman sitting around in supreme confidence on the couch in her knickers and bra in front of other men after she has satisfied all of them. I think it is because it has shown the power and strength she has as a woman. She can see all the guys are exhausted and she has handled them with ease. We are all sexual beings and having the ability to express that is exciting and liberating for both men and women. It lightens up your life and, like anything else, it must be kept in perspective and it shouldn't dominate your life. Sex is a small part of life that can have a big effect on a large part of your life though, whether we like it or not.

## Ladies, you won't be alone if you accept men for the sexual animals they are

When it comes to the sexual side of their life, all men dream of having an erotic woman who will do anything he wants. We men are simple creatures, so why on earth would you ever risk a marriage or a relationship on the simple action of keeping his tummy full, his balls empty and his ego in good shape.

If that makes men sound pathetic, that's because we are pathetic, when it comes to sex.

Just as, "love is part of a man's life but all of a woman's life", "Sex is part of a woman's life but all of a man's life" and that's where the conflict comes from.

Any woman who understands and caters for the primal, sexual side of men will never be alone. Conversely, women who don't understand men sexually will always lose if they go up against a woman who is aware of, and caters for, the primal sexual side of her man. Losing out on a happy life is a big sacrifice to make over not catering for the primal sexual side of men. Girls want the world to be a fairy tale and are disgusted by the primal sexual side of men whereas women accept it, understand it and give their man what they need to keep them happy and keep them there.

## Men – you won't be alone if you free the sexuality of your woman

A lot of men remain boys all their life. They never really enjoy women, in a sexual sense, because they are indiscrete, judgemental and hypocritical. They have the vestal virgin and the whore mindset. The wife is at home being the Vestal Virgin whilst they are out of town screwing hookers (70% of married men have had sex with a hooker).

Men, on the other hand, understand that all women are both Vestal Virgins and whores. It's all just a matter of timing. These men really enjoy everything about their woman and allow her to reveal her sexual personality in a trusting and discrete environment. As a general rule, I have found women to be far more sexually adventurous than men given the right environment. They are more in touch with their bodies and more sensual. If you allow your partner to express herself sexually a whole new world will open up to you. If you don't, a man who does may meet her some day and fuck her or, worse, she'll leave you for him. Women will never reveal their sexuality; you need to draw it out of them. If you do that then she will never leave you because of want and variety in a sexual sense.

If you have never thought about this, as a man, I promise you that there is a whole secret erotic world out there that is open to you if you are discrete, non-judgemental man who is open and aware of female sexuality.

## Why sex will never be the cause of problems in this happy marriage

This book has been all about sex and yet it's not really about sex at all.

This book is about getting sex into perspective and having a plan to control and direct it so you can sustain the far more important and lasting wonders of life such as love, trust and a happy family.

Instead of random sexual acts, which can happen at the wrong place and the wrong time, we decided to guarantee that anything we did would not have any chance of interfering with the people we love and the happy marriage we enjoy.

There is no chance of my wife or I ever having a secret sexual affair and the chance of our marriage breaking up over sexually related issues is absolutely zero.

In truth, because we both know we can do anything we want, we have gone full circle and don't have many sexual adventures these days. We are like kids in a candy store who have enough money to buy everything but are mature enough to do things in moderation.

Sexual freedom for us has made us more innocent in our everyday life too. People we meet think we are a newly married couple and are surprised to hear we have been together for over 25 years. Our marriage is fresh and fun, and we are always affectionate and loving towards each other because we have enjoyed discrete adventures together in our own secret little world. I think being free of suppressed sexual desires has allowed us to feel free and relaxed in the way we live our day to day lives.

## Marriage is still a beautiful thing

People love getting married and being married. Why else would so many people get married even when they know that half of all marriages end in divorce. Our personal experience has shown that the marriage model, based on the model of 2350 BC can still work, but it does work better with a few updates. We updated our marriage to acknowledge the freedom of choice that is available to every couple today. We felt strange about trying this at first, but it works.

I hope that the experiences we have shared here will, in some way, give you and the ones you love a happier and more relaxed life.

www.ingramcontent.com/pod-product-compliance
Lightning Source LLC
Chambersburg PA
CBHW060502280326
41933CB00014B/2832